Under Five Flags

by
Hackchan Rhee and
Marta L. Tullis

DORRANCE PUBLISHING CO
EST. 1920
PITTSBURGH, PENNSYLVANIA 15238

The contents of this work, including, but not limited to, the accuracy of events, people, and places depicted; opinions expressed; permission to use previously published materials included; and any advice given or actions advocated are solely the responsibility of the author, who assumes all liability for said work and indemnifies the publisher against any claims stemming from publication of the work.

All Rights Reserved
Copyright © 2016 by Hackchan Rhee and Marta L. Tullis

No part of this book may be reproduced or transmitted, downloaded, distributed, reverse engineered, or stored in or introduced into any information storage and retrieval system, in any form or by any means, including photocopying and recording, whether electronic or mechanical, now known or hereinafter invented without permission in writing from the publisher.

Dorrance Publishing Co
585 Alpha Drive
Suite 103
Pittsburgh, PA 15238
Visit our website at *www.dorrancebookstore.com*

ISBN: 978-1-4809-3379-8
eISBN: 978-1-4809-3356-9

Chapter I
Sungchun Leaves Home

*I*n early December 1915, a young boy named Sungchun, born in June 1902, left his home in a small farm town, Yonggang-Onchon, approximately thirty miles from Pyongyang, and walked toward Pyongyang with hope that he would be able to pursue his education and build a successful career in the second largest city of Korea. In those bitterly cold days, he walked through mountain trails, crossing rivers from sunrise to sundown. The reason for his leaving his home at the age of thirteen was that the family was very poor (they were tenant farmers, obliged to share income from the property with the landlord), and they had a hard time feeding and clothing him, especially during the hard times that had prevailed during World War I. Although their lot was not unusual for those days, starvation loomed large in those years when crops failed. Even successful years did not bring a great deal of money, and feeding and clothing an extra person was a real hardship. Sungchun's parents were capable of working the farm, in combination with his younger brother, and the loss of the older son's assistance could be borne better than his constant presence. Any inherited money from Sungchun's grandparents was also about to become exhausted. Pyongyang, therefore, represented both an opportunity for a better life and escape from the daily, grinding poverty that had so worn his parents down.

The trip was exceptionally difficult for him. He did not have many warm clothes or proper dress or any money. Two days after his departure, he ran into a heavy snow blizzard on the narrow, mountain road, and there was not a single house or shelter within the next two to three miles. By then he had consumed all the food that his mother had packed for him when he left home, and he was very hungry. The trail became invisible from the snowfall. It was seven at night, but the surroundings were relatively light from the reflection of the snow on the ground. He was beginning to regret leaving his parents. The steady sound of wind swept through the pine leaves, and mounting darkness made him think that he was the only soul on earth living.

Suddenly he saw a weak light spot across the hillside. He became wide awake and roused himself toward the light spot that he hoped was a farmhouse.

Undoubtedly it was a farmhouse with a couple of workers who were working late to produce candy syrups to make candy the next day. Sungchun was too exhausted to shout for help. After a few tentative knocks at the front door, which got the worker's attention, he collapsed on his knees and barely opened his eyes and tried to reach the workers' hands. They held the thirteen-year-old boy in their arms and rushed into the quarters and laid him on the warm floor and covered him with layers of quilts. The boy subconsciously made sounds through the ice around his lips and the frost around his scarf but soon fell asleep. At sunrise the next morning, he woke up and discovered that he was lying in someone's house with quilts on top and surrounded by two women and two husky looking men, who were the occupants of the house. Later he was introduced to the staff and their wives, as well as the owner of the candy factory. Sungchun expressed his gratefulness for their help and was ready to continue his journey. The farmers shouted at him, "You must stay awhile until you have recovered. Eat your soup. It's warm and will make you think better and help you recover from your exhaustion." After a few days, Sungchun was strong enough to take a few steps outside the door and checked the weather to see if he could continue his journey without running into another snowstorm. The sun was very bright, and the air was crispy cold and fresh. He then realized that he was only a day-and-a-half walking distance away from Pyongyang. He told the owner that he would be leaving after helping them with their chores as a means of paying back their hospitality. The owner answered, "We do not expect you to pay back anything, but we want you to stay here through the winter and earn some money for your initial living expenses at Pyongyang." Sungchun then gratefully took their advice and halted his journey until early April the following year.

Chapter II
Why Sungchun Left Home — Environmental Influences

*A*s noted in the previous chapter, Sungchun came to leave home simply because at the time when he left, Korea was an economic basket case, and its inhabitants had an extremely difficult time making a living, with few prospects for a brighter future. Since time immemorial, Korea has been at a disadvantage because of its geography. Its location as a peninsula in an extreme northern latitude has made it prone to extremes of temperature, quite hot in the summer due to the tropical wind pattern from the South Pacific and very cold in the winter due to the Arctic wind pattern from Siberia in the north. Its location between Manchuria in the north, Japan in the southeast, China in the northwest, Russia in its occupied southern portion of Manchuria and Siberia across the northeastern border of Korea, and Mongolia in the west have made it an easy target for invading armies to loot and plunder, not only for its rich natural reserves of copper, lead, gold, coal, and iron ore, but also for the fact that its location allowed it to be used as a bridge for the conflicts between the surrounding powerful nations. Consequently its name as the "Hermit Kingdom" arose in light of the fact that Koreans have been among the most insular people in the world, suspicious of outsiders and their intentions.

Koreans are known as industrious, highly competitive, and highly conscious about personal hygiene, as well as being nature lovers. Because the climate is extremely hot in the summer and extremely cold in the winter, they maintain their physical toughness and also choose to eat hot and spicy food in order to get themselves warm in a winter climate. Koreans are a people who move and think fast and are very conscious of physical cleanliness. They are clean because of the ready availability of water. Approximately 70 percent of Korea is mountainous, and there are plenty of mountain streams flowing everywhere. They are competitive because their country has been invaded numerous times by surrounding powerful nations: China, Manchuria, Mongolia, and Japan. For this reason, they have become strong fighters against the foreign invaders. The Americans, for example, were not able to defeat the North Koreans during the Korean War. Also during the Vietnam War, President Nixon selected a South Korean infantry division to fight in Vietnam. They were able to defeat many North Vietnamese strongholds during the war. During the 1936 Nazi Olympics at Berlin, Sohn Kee-Chung of Korea won the gold medal in the marathon. There is a legendary story that Sohn was supposedly representing Japan and wearing a Japanese flag on his chest, but that Syngman Rhee, who was leading the temporary Korean independence movement in the U.S., and his followers ripped off the Japanese flag and replaced it with the Korean flag (Taegukgi) prior to the award ceremony. The Japanese authorities forcefully replaced it back with their flag thereafter. While I have been unable to verify the truth of this story, at least one newspaper, *Dong Ailbo*, carried a photo of Sohn Kee-Chung with the Japanese flag scratched out. Shortly thereafter the paper was shut down for months and eight of its journalists tortured.[1] In 1983 in testing sponsored by the Educational Testing Service in Washington, Korean students scored first in math and science tests of eighth graders among 24,000 students from six nations, including the U.S., Britain, Ireland, Canada, and Spain.[2]

Koreans are also highly innovative. They installed the world's first planetary observatory tower, Cheomseongdae Observatory (star-gazing tower), in the reign of Queen Seon-deok (632–674), which still exists in South Korea. Also the first Asian sundial, water-powered clocks, and astronomical maps and atlases of the seven planets were produced during King Sejong's era (1418-1450)[3,4]. During the Koryo Dynasty in 1232, metal, movable type was invented, and it supplanted the woodblock printing originally introduced from China.[5] During the Japanese invasion of Korea (1592-1598) led by the Japanese warlord Toyotomi Hideyoshi, who had the ambition of conquering Ming

China with Portuguese guns, the Choson Dynasty built the first cannon-bearing, ironclad warships in world history, called Kobuk Sun, meaning "turtle ship." They repelled the invasion by the Japanese Navy, ending the seven-year-long war in 1598. During that war, Toyotomi Hideyoshi committed atrocities against the Korean people and terrorized them by chopping off the heads of Korean combatants and shipping the heads back to Japan. Eventually he found it easier to just chop off the noses and ears of the Korean casualties.

The power of Confucian philosophy can be seen in various aspects of Korean legend and history. For example, when Yi Soon Shin went to see the Korean emperor King Joong Jong for the first time, he wrote in Chinese characters, "He who would save his life will lose it, and he who would lose his life will save it." This is also very comparable to the New Testament teachings of Jesus, who said, "He who would save his life will lose it, and he who would lose his life will save it."[6]

Koreans are very observant and critical about many things. They tend to criticize others without much hesitation. Likewise their language consists of many adjectives and adverbs. For example, they do not just say "beautiful"; there are many different kinds of "beautifulness" in their language.

The name of the country Korea is derived from the Koryo Dynasty, which lasted over four hundred years from 918 until the generals of Yi Songae (or Seonggye) and Choe Yeong ousted the Koryo Dynasty.[7] General Yi then established the Yi Dynasty (or Choson Dynasty) beginning in 1392, which lasted through 1910. Prior to the formation of the Koryo Dynasty, Korea was divided into three kingdoms: Koguryo (which includes nearly all the southern half of Manchuria, currently known as Eastern China), Silla, and Paekche.

Silla was the most civilized nation and created many cultural items and art objects. Koguryo was the most powerful and established many diplomatic channels throughout Asia and the Mideast. During the Koryo Dynasty, the world famous "Cheongja" porcelains were produced.[8] At the same time, the potters invented techniques that produced brilliant and elegant effects, such as Celadon glazes that were much admired by the Chinese and Japanese.[9] Currently North Korea is called "Cho-Seon..." (朝鮮...), which is carried over from the name "Choson Dynasty." South Korea has been called Hankuk, which is the adaptation of the name "Great Imperial Nation Han"(大韓帝國), since 1897.

One might ask, "In spite of all these splendid inventions made by Koreans and their individual superiority, why has the country never become one of the leading, powerful nations of Asia?" Generally there are several reasons for this, but it is largely due to a lack of certain resources (particularly oil) and that the people often do not work well together in a group (one of their chief distinctions from the Japanese). Because of their great competitiveness, they are very jealous toward one other's success and prosperity. The current political situation of a divided Korea since the end of WWII demonstrates this. Many influences from other powerful nations, including the former Soviet Union, have been a contributing factor for maintaining the division of Korea to the present day. On the other hand, the strategies of in the past few years as the generation of people and their families who were separated by the Korean War (North and South) are gradually dying off, it seems that the leaders of both countries shy away from any sense of urgency for reunification of the two divided countries.

Traditionally Koreans have loved quietness, the theatre, sad stories, and music that sounds sad because the history of Korea has been one in which their crops and other resources have been robbed by surrounding nations, including the Manchu (1636-1637), Qing China (late sixteenth thru early seventeenth centuries), and the Japanese — both since the period of annexation in 1910 as well as during the time of the warlord Toyotomi Hideyoshi, who retreated from Korea in 1598.[10] The Toyotomi regime was notoriously brutal. It not only took farming and mining resources but also killed or kidnapped thousands of Korean inventors and skilled workers, including the Celadon glaze makers, back to Japan.[11] There was a legendary story that the warlord Hideyoshi was brought low by the cunning and offices of a Korean geisha girl. The warlord was extremely paranoid, especially regarding his sleeping arrangements. He had evidently learned the technique of sleeping with his eyes wide open while surrounded by cowbells attached to a loop of strings. When the Koreans felt it was time to kill the warlord, they enlisted the help of the Korean geisha to stuff the cowbells full of cotton and allow at least one soldier near the general's bed. The soldier chopped off the general's head, but fearing his reputed mystic powers, which they feared would enable him to reattach his head instantaneously, they had the geisha standing by with an apron full of ashes, which she immediately flung onto the general's headless neck, preventing the head from reattaching. Once he was satisfied that the general was well and truly dead, the soldier's attention was drawn to the geisha.

"We know you are pregnant with the warlord's child," said the soldier. "Would you be willing to sacrifice yourself for the sake of Korea?"

"Do I have any choice?" replied the geisha.

With that, a single, swift stroke of the soldier's sword opened up the geisha's belly. Out came a three-month-old fetus, who said to the soldier, "If you had let me lie another six months, I would have killed you the day I was born!"

As mentioned earlier, such invasions by other nations led Korea to a rigid, isolationist policy, for which the country became known as the "Hermit Kingdom." One of the most commonly used expression among Koreans at times of hardship or any depression due to his/her living conditions is "아이고죽겠다, 아이고죽겠어!" (aigozhukaltta, aigozhukasso") which is essentially interpreted as "Oh I wish I was dead!" At thirteen years of age, Sungchun probably had the same sort of feelings about his living conditions, as well as for his future, and finally decided to leave home.

Korea's location between Russian and Manchuria in the north, Japan in the south, and China in the northwest made Korea a tempting target for the empire-building strategies of these countries since the end of the nineteenth century. The Korean royal house had long striven to fend off outside influences and maintain absolute control of its subjects. It had tried to keep abreast of world developments as best it could, largely through the reports and good offices of those Koreans who had traveled abroad and had obtained some education and influence in the outside world. I have paid homage to the grave of one of those patriots, Park Hee Byung, a Korean patriot who died mysteriously in Denver, Colorado, in 1907. He had originally traveled to the United States to obtain a mining engineering degree in the company of one of the emperor's sons and had been drawn to the Denver area due to the extremely busy and profitable conditions in Colorado which existed at the turn of the century. He attempted to build support for a resolution to be presented at the 1908 Democratic National Convention that would have called upon the Japanese to vacate their colonial presence in Korea. As the circumstances of his death were never adequately explained, it was rumored that he was assassinated by agents of the neighboring country, inasmuch as Park Hee Byung's burial location was not identified until 2003, when the South Korean government decided to place a headstone on his grave. (Interestingly his nephew, Park Yong-Man, went to Kearney, Nebraska, (near my original alma mater in the U.S., Hastings College) and set up a military training camp to train fighters to attack the Japanese. Paradoxically Park Yong-Man was assassinated in 1928 in Beijing by a Korean communist who believed he was an agent of the Japanese. The sight of Park Hee Byung's grave was heart-wrenching. Although the tombstone erected in 2007 by the Denver Korean Consulate is quite impressive and details the circumstances of his death, it is the sole memorial in the pauper's section of the cemetery. Stark and austere, the grave nonetheless has immense power by virtue of its size and majesty, as well as its relative isolation.

The Korean monarchy had been prodded at home toward a more enlightened government by such early reformers as Syngman Rhee (born in 1875 and later the president of South Korea from 1948-1960), who had been thrown into prison by the Yi Dynasty in 1897 for taking part in a protest against the monarchy. He was released in 1904 and fled to the U.S., where he obtained several degrees relating to political science, including a Ph.D. from Princeton University in international law. He attempted to influence the United States government to press the cause of Korean reform and to permit a more democratic government to exist. However, Korea had entered into an alliance with Japan for defensive purposes against a Russian invasion prior to the 1904 Russo-Japanese war. Seeking to use the defensive treaty as authority to use Korea as a colonial base of operations, the Japanese began to encroach upon Korean territory. As his kingdom began to crumble, King Kojong (renamed as "emperor" since 1897), recognized his tenuous position and eventually took refuge in the Russian consulate, leaving Queen Min, who had been endeavoring to obtain Russian support for the Korean throne, to fend for herself in the royal palace. At the dawn of October 8, 1895, she was eventually assassinated by Miura Goro, the Japanese minister to Korea, and some of his government officials. The three beautiful and relatively older ladies who were also killed by the assassins inside the palace effectively obscured the identity of the real Queen Min until the prince (Queen Min's son) and the court's ladies-in-waiting identified the real Queen Min after they had been shown the faces of victims. The body of Queen Min was burned by gasoline poured over the body inside the courtyard by the Japanese assassins.[12] The remaining members of the royal family were eventually brought under Japanese influence and divested of their royal power. The power vacuum thus created eventually permitted the Japanese to declare Korea as a Japanese colony and to use Korea as a base for their dynastic aspirations involving the extension of the Japanese empire further into Asia.

Although the Japanese did not officially invade Korea until 1907, with the exception of the Japan-Sino War (1894) that had occurred in the northern region of Korea, including Pyongyang, they had been sending émigrés, such as the ex-Samurais or the criminals of the Japanese homeland to Korea for some years. Since the inception of the Meiji regime, Japan had looked outward toward Asia as a means of obtaining raw materials that were scarce at home and for fulfilling what they believed was their "manifest destiny," i.e., to take over most of Asia and to have Asian resources, as well as its people, at their disposal. Further, the spread of communism eastward, following the spread of capitalistic colonialism, from the heart of Europe struck fear into the heart of the Japanese, who were both highly traditional and intensely capitalistic in their service to the emperor.

As was mentioned in previous chapter, Sungchun was born in 1902 and left home at age thirteen (which would have put him in Pyongyang sometime in 1916). It was during this time that the Korean royal house, which had been effectively overthrown by the Japanese military, was being reduced to the status of a puppet regime, with little autonomy and few rights. Naturally the condition of the whole of Korea followed suit. For this reason, the Japanese, propelled by their desire for continental expansion, had selected Korea as their base of operations on the continent of Asia. They were not prepared to brook any opposition to their expansionist plans, which involved the industrialization of Northern Korea, including the exploitation of iron and coal mines and the building of an extensive railway system that left Korea with more railway track per square mile than any other nation on earth. During the Japanese occupation, they had built outstanding industrial facilities (which were the largest in Asia), such as the steel refinery in Pyongan Province, the hydroelectric power dam on the Yalu River at the border between Manchuria and Korea, and the corn mill in Pyongyang. The seizure of farmland in the south meant that Japanese farmers and fishermen were given Korean farmland or allowed to purchase it for a nominal fee while the original Korean owners were reduced to sharecropper status or fled to Manchuria in search of a better life.[13]

Rapid industrialization did not bring immediate prosperity to the Korean people. The Japanese acquisition of important natural resources, together with the creation of public-works projects, created dislocations within Korean society that were not, in some cases, easy to absorb. Riots occurred together with strikes and demonstrations, which were put down with customary efficiency by the Japanese-controlled police, military police, and Japanese royal troops. It was against this backdrop that Sungchun was employed by a Japanese watchmaker as a janitor/junior technician in Pyongyang. As he was a minor, it was not unusual that he became unskilled labor as soon as he reached Pyongyang. The watchmaker was one of the Japanese settlers to Pyongyang after Korea was formally annexed to Japan. In exchange for his service, Sungchun was given free room and board. The watchmaker appeared to have taken a real paternal interest in the young boy, as he ensured that Sungchun had an opportunity to go to school and build a better future. In addition to providing room, board, and necessities, the Japanese watchmaker enabled him to go to obtain some additional training (probably via a middle school or perhaps on-the-job training), where he learned some aspects of civil engineering that enabled him to take over the flow-meter repair section at the city water department.

Theoretically under the Japanese school system, middle school was known as "gymnasium" — in combination with the curriculums learned in engineering, accounting, and other professional fields. His education enabled him to eventually obtain a role in the Pyongyang city water department's repair shop (mainly repairing and testing water-flow meters) as a supervisor, which was facilitated by the watchmaker through his contacts in the Japanese administration at Pyongyang city hall.

While Sungchun was working for the watchmaker and attending school, however, much of Korea was seething in unrest. Several major incidents had occurred, such as unfair court trials and judgments by the Japanese military police against Korean defendants; loss of sovereign power within the Hankuk Imperial palace; the new land investigation work initiated by the Japanese governor-general of Korea; the establishment of new educational objectives to convert Korean students to loyalty to the Japanese emperor; enforcing the use of Japanese language in preference to the Korean language in schools and businesses; and the burning of Korean history books with gasoline in the streets of major cities. Furthermore the death of the former Hankuk Emperor

Kozong made Koreans suspicious that the emperor was poisoned by the Japanese authorities. At the First World War peace treaty in Paris in January 1919, the exiled Korean delegate from Shanghai unsuccessfully submitted a document requesting the recognition of Korea as an independent nation.[14]

Tragedy struck when the great earthquake in Japan occurred on Sept. 1, 1923. As a result of the devastation and the extensive loss of life, many of the Japanese killed the Koreans in their midst. The Koreans were blamed for contaminated water and the fire that broke out through Tokyo. Most allegations were untrue, but the blame remained in place. Some Japanese students were mistaken for Koreans and were killed by mistake. To prevent future occurrences, the Japanese would make the captured students attempt to reproduce the "r" sound. If he did not do so in the classic Japanese sound, he was killed.[15] In contrast to this, Koreans have a much better pronunciation of r's and l's, as demonstrated by the song of the drunken Yang Ban who walked into the lake, mistaking the reflection of the moon on the lake for the moon itself. The name of the song is "O Moon."

Koreans continued resisting at an accelerating pace. A riot that occurred on March 1, 1919, fueled the "Samil" Movement, which was put down under Japan's martial law by the Japanese police, military police, and troops of the army and navy. The movement was initiated by Korean students in Japan on February 8 submitting a declaration of independence to the Japanese government and proceeding with a demonstration march. On March 1, 1919, two days prior to the funeral of Emperor Kozong, leaders of a few religious organizations gathered in the Taehwa Gwan building in Seoul and read the declaration of independence. Soon followed by students reading the declaration of independence at Topgol Park in Seoul in front of several thousand citizens and students, they continued with a demonstration march in the city. Within a few days, the independence movement expanded throughout many cities of Korea, with nearly two million students, farmers, laborers and merchants participating. The number of casualties resulting from this movement was listed at 7,509 deaths, including 15,961 wounded and 15,961 arrested. It was estimated that the total number of buildings burned by Japanese troops was 715 residential houses, 47 churches and 2 schools.[16]

After the violent protests unleashed by the Proclamation of Independence, Syngman Rhee continued his activities campaigning for Korean independence while he was based in Hawaii and also in 1919 when he was named as the president of the Korean provisional government in exile at Shanghai. Although he was impeached by the Provisional Assembly in 1925, he continued with his work in the U.S., attempting to persuade the League of Nations to place the Korean government in receivership. He was ultimately named head of the provisional government in Korea.

In the Andong province of Manchuria, some of the exiled Koreans prepared for a war of independence.[17]Kim Il-Sung, whose namesake appeared as "the Great Leader"(prime minister of North Korea (1948-1972) and president of North Korea (1972-1994)), initially joined an underground Marxist organization. Thereafter he joined a guerrilla group led by the Communist Party of China. Later Kim and other Korean Communist guerrillas were retrained by the Soviet army at camp near Khabarovsk, and according to legend, they raided many small-scale Japanese military camps in Manchuria and in the northeastern mountain region of Korea (Hamgyong Bukto Province).[18] The guerrilla force was known as "Palzzisan" or "Pal-lo-gun," roughly translating as "partisan" or "Soviet affiliated troop." Although both Syngman Rhee and Kim Il-Sung were rumored to have participated in the Samil Movement, I have not been able to verify that either of them actually participated in this movement. Certainly neither man's name appears on the Proclamation of Independence that was declared in Topgol Park in Seoul. After the violent protests unleashed by the Proclamation of Independence, Kim Il-Sung went deep into the mountains of Manchuria and fought against the Japanese there.

Although Sungchun was aware of the Korean resistance to its Japanese masters, he did not act against them, probably because they had been kind and helpful to him. Furthermore he then was in Manchuria to attend middle school (gymnasium) sponsored by the Japanese watchmaker. He apparently escaped the wrath of the populace, who turned against many others who had also been closely connected with the Japanese and had profited thereby.

Endnotes
1. Andy Bull, "The Sports Blog," *The Guardian.co.uk*, August 27, 2011.
2. Knight Ridder News Service-Washington, *Denver Post*, 1983.
3. "Joseon," http://en.wikipedia.org/wiki/Joseon_Dynasty.
4. https: en.wikipedia.org/wiki/Sejong_the_Great

5. See note 3 above.
6. Yi Soon Shin videotapes, vol. II, disk 3, episode 25.

   Biblical references:

   John 12:15, "He who loves his life loses it, and he who hates his life in this world will keep it for eternal life."

   Luke 17:33, "Whoever seeks to gain his life will lose it, but whoever loses his life will preserve it."

   Mark 8:35, "For whoever would save his life will lose it; and whoever loses his life for my sake and the gospel's will save it."

   Matthew 10:39, "He who finds his life will lose it, and he who loses his life for my sake will find it."
7. See Note 3
8. https: // en.wikipedia.org/wiki/Korean_pottery_and_porcelain
9. S. Kuliak and, J. Clarke, ed., "Museum Guide," (The Art Institute of Chicago, 1992).
10. //https: en.wikipedia.org/wiki/Turtle_ship
11. See note 8 above.
12. Hiroshi Aoki, *Recent History of Japan, China and Korea*, (Japan: Gentosha, 2003), 33-34, 53-57, 65. (日本、中口、朝鮮；近現代史；青木裕司)
13. "History of Korea," www.k365.com/history/81.htm .
14. See note 12 above.
15. See note 12 above.
16. https: //en.wikipedia.org/wiki/March_1st_movement
17. https: //en.wikipedia.org/wiki/Kim Il-Sung
18. See note 17 above

Chapter III
New Beginnings — Sungchun Grows Up,
Gets a Job, and Starts a Family

*A*s mentioned in Chapter II, my father had been employed by a Japanese watchmaker, an émigré from Japan, since arriving in Pyongyang in 1915. The watchmaker had been one of the settlers who had arrived in Japan since the Japanese invaded Korea and formally annexed Korea to Japan, which had occurred in 1910. Although he had been able to receive free room and board, as well as an education up through middle school, my father felt concern for his parents and wondered what had become of them. He wanted to let them know he had done relatively well and felt himself in a better position to try to alleviate their poverty, if they required it.

They were pleased to see him and were gratified to know that he had indeed done well, as they had heard nothing from him in the preceding ten years. But they were sorry to inform him that his younger brother, Song, had died some years earlier, having swallowed a poisonous tincture made from a poisonous snake and pickled in sake in an effort to cure a huge swelling on the side of his neck (probably a goiter). Before he returned to Pyongyang, they introduced him to yet another future member of the family — that is, his future wife, my mother.

In those days, marriages were often arranged by families for their children. Casual dating was unheard of, largely in response to the dictates of Confucius, who had decreed that "boys and girls should not be left alone together past the age of six years." Although free to reject the family's selection, both men and women were expected to consider the future spouse's relationship to the rest of the family and ensure that he or she would blend well with other relatives and could live with and help support the aging parents. Ancient tradition also dictated that one's spouse would remain in the family — not only through life but in death. Although the ancient spirit traditions of Korea have largely been supplanted by modern thought and Christianity, remarriage of widows remained uncommon until well past the beginning of the twentieth century. Widows traditionally have been expected to maintain their widowhood, devoting themselves to their families until death. So it was not at all unusual for my father to have met and married my mother at the request of his parents, even though he had known her only a little while at the time. Fortunately the marriage went well and produced me; my sister, Heechan; and my brothers, Youngchan and Inchon. Only Youngchan and I survived the Korean War; the rest of the family has never been heard from since we left Korea shortly after the war.

When my father returned home to visit my grandparents after having lived for years in Pyongyang, my grandparents decided that it was time my father got married. They consulted with a local matchmaker, who was one member of an informal network throughout the area. The matchmaker knew that my mother was available and took it upon herself to visit with my mother's parents. In early spring of 1924, my father and his parents came to my mother's house to interview her as a prospective bride. Mother was born on January 1, 1906, in the lunar calendar in the same coastal town where Uncle Kim lived — Hanchon, Pyungnam province, which is approximately forty miles from Pyongyang. She was eighteen when she married Father. She hailed from a reasonably respectable family. Her father was a physician practicing ancient Chinese medicine. Mother's parents kindly prepared much delicious food and led them into their guest room. The interview conversations were mostly limited to their genetic background of origin. They determined that Mother's family had originated from the Eu clan of Hanchon province, whereas Father's family originated from the Rhee (or Yi) clan of Zonzu province. It was customary then, as it is today, to assure that prospective marriage partners are sufficiently distantly related to prevent birth defects or mental retardation. Further my mother's parents questioned the groom about his job and his income and future prospects. After about an hour interview, they left the guest room and left the two young persons alone in the room. For a moment, the two young people were very reluctant to talk freely about anything, except to express to one another repeatedly how glad they were to meet each other. Finally, the groom found himself getting wrapped up in discussion of his early work and experience at the Japanese watch repair shop in Pyongyang and his prospects with the city water department. My father must have been sufficiently charming and persuasive, and my mother sufficiently attractive, because at the end of the meeting, they announced their tentative engagement. The engagement became finalized after three months, which allowed time for the elaborate wedding preparations. They were married at my mother's home, although they had not seen one another since their initial meeting until three days prior to the wedding. Wedding customs dictate a remarkably simple ceremony; there are no vows between husband and wife, merely bowing to one another across a table is considered sufficient to indicate their consent to matrimony, although signatures on a marriage certificate are usually required by the government. The wife's status within the household is very much subject to her husband's dictates; there is no word for "wife" in the Korean language — rather the word for "corner person" is used. Korean adults did not usually call one another by their first names. This was true even for husbands and wives, who referred to one another with the equivalent of Mr. and Mrs., together with their respective surnames. The wife did not usually take her husband's last name.

Wedding gifts in Korea tend to be simple, and in the case of food gifts, even live. My father mentioned that he was the recipient of several live chickens, as well as at least one beef roast on his wedding day. The celebration went on all night, with the drunken wedding guests beseeching my father and mother to begin by shaking hands. After my mother reluctantly shook hands with him, she was then commanded to kiss my father. Being bashful she was reluctant at first but finally agreed. The final straw, however, came when my father refused to provide any more alcohol to his already inebriated guests. They thereupon suspended him from the ceiling until he agreed to provide more drinks!

Upon Father and Mother's marriage, they immediately returned to Pyongyang and spent a short time in Father's old room with the watchmaker until such time as they could locate a suitable house to buy, which Father's new position as the manager of the city water department's test and repair shop made possible. They eventually located a house within Pyongyang and moved out to begin their independent new life and to start a family.

The house they located was old and in need of repair. In the tradition of the American "starter house," Father set about repairing the old house (mostly providing new plaster and bracing to the walls, which were often made of corn stalks and scrap wood, and providing updates to the porch floors) in order to make it more attractive and livable. During their married life, it was the pattern for Father to move into an old house that required fixing up. He improved and renovated it and moved on to the next fixer-upper. Father renovated several houses in this manner, each time selling them at a good profit, the money thus obtained being turned over to Mother to invest.

Mother invested money and handled all our financial affairs even though she only had a sixth grade education, which was usual for women of those days. All money resulting from the turnover in our homes went into her capable hands for investment into real estate. She economized in various ways, from planting a garden, sewing her own clothes, and buying our clothes at the local penitentiary. The money she saved by these means also went into purchasing land as an investment, with my father's cousin working the land. At the end, she had managed to acquire nearly forty acres of farmland near Yong Gang.

The land was planted in barley, milo, corn, and soybeans. The barley was used for direct human consumption; milo was used for animal feed, mostly for pigs. Korean milo is tall, whereas Nebraska milo is short. Yellow rice is produced on dry land and was bought by poor people. Corn was used for both animal and human consumption and was brought to Korea by American missionaries. The corn was especially profitable and was bought by the local corn processing plant in order to produce meal, medicine, and corn flour. The profits from the sale of corn enabled some of our fields to be planted in apples rather than corn. However, when the Russians came, they stole all our apples and chopped down the trees, saying that the apples were a luxury that the Koreans could ill-afford, and ordered that the fields be replanted in grains as they had been before.

Children resulting from this marriage included an older sister who died when she was 1½ years old, myself (Hackchan, whose name means splendid scholar), Youngchan (splendid hero), Inchon (tiger, so called because he enjoyed eating raw meat in his early days), and Heechan (splendid angel).

My older sister lived and died before I was born. She was born in 1927 and died at 1½ years old. According to my grandmother's story, she died of a severe "charley horse" while she was playing in the front yard. Her entire arms and legs were crimped and stiffened and caused her immediate death. I do not know exactly what caused such a tragedy, but it was not uncommon for infant children to die suddenly in Korea in those days. Many parents took preventive measures against early death by burning locally on the crown of the child's head at a young age in the event of illness. Although this rather drastic measure sometimes seemed to work, the downside of this meant that the skull burns, which were approximately ¾-inch in diameter, remained on the child's head for the rest of his or her life.

I was the oldest living child, having been born on December 24, 1928 (lunar calendar), which equates to February 3, 1929, in the solar calendar. I was a sickly child and required much care and attention during my early years. Since my childhood, however, I have rarely been sick and have been able to maintain good health.

My brother Youngchan was closest in age to me, having been born on May 6, 1932. Youngchan is the only brother I escaped with together from North Korea to South Korea in December 1950 as refugees. I suspect he is the only other member of the family who survived the war. He is the only relative with whom I have associated with since then.

My sister Heechan was born in 1935, and although I do not remember the exact date, it was sometime in October. She was a lovely girl and father's pet, which made me jealous at times. Her life with three brothers could not have been easy, but she took it in good part most of the time, only breaking into tears of frustration and rage on rare occasions. Her nerves were delicate, however, and as the political situation in North Korea deteriorated, she refused to go to school, claiming she couldn't handle the stress.

My brother Inchon, who was my favorite, was born in 1938. He was sufficiently distant in age to present any threat, besides which he was the most like me. He and I were always striving to excel in both school and athletics, and he looked up to me as the elder brother without challenging my authority.

My father had a rather distinguished career at the city water department of Pyongyang, which controlled the water from the Ta Dong River, as well as the streams that trickled down from the mountains surrounding Pyongyang. He became the head of the city water department's repair shop under the Japanese, which was one of the most important positions attainable by a Korean under the Japanese administration. He was well-liked and respected by both his Korean employees as well as his Japanese employers. He was fairly secure in that post, which was a blessing to him, as even under the Japanese, the economics of Korea were uncertain. Although well-positioned, he could not always avoid or shelter his family from the rapid changes in the political and economic climate that were transpiring in Korea. Although our family was relatively well-positioned within the social structure, there were nevertheless sudden occurrences which threatened to disrupt our family or its standing within the community. One such occurrence was when my father risked his position with the city water department, and possibly his life, in order to come to the aid of some Chinese neighbors.

Immigrant Chinese who had settled in Pyongyang and who had made themselves prosperous through their hard work in tilling the unproductive soil near the regions that adjoined Pyongyang were being persecuted with some frequency, probably due to the jealousy of the native Koreans, who envied them their financial well-being. On one occasion, my father had occasion to save an immigrant Chinese family from being attacked by enraged Koreans and managed to get them to safety behind the walls of a local Christian missionary compound. As it turned out, the Chinese were also Christian (Presbyterian), and the local missionaries were very grateful to my father for having saved the Chinese family. My father was asked if he had ever thought of going to America. He replied no, but in the forthcoming years, he increasingly thought about such a possibility. He had a great deal of respect for the missionaries and their lifestyle, especially the educational opportunities that the missionaries offered. He eventually lost contact with the missionaries, who probably went back to the U.S. prior to WWII.

Chapter IV
Growing Up in Korea

*G*rowing up in Korea during the 1930s and 1940s was most challenging — and somewhat dangerous. However, this time period was the link between the current modern era and the ancient ways that had served Korea for centuries — in some cases well and in other cases badly. Being spectator to this metamorphosis was sometimes gratifying, sometimes frightening, but always interesting.

Our family was reasonably prosperous and well-off compared to our neighbors, who in many cases did not have especially well-paying jobs or who may have been unemployed. As previously related, our renovation and sale of successive houses in Pyongyang permitted us to acquire a fairly substantial amount of money. As these houses were not always located in the safest or choicest areas of the city, there was perhaps more crime and exposure to poverty than would have been the case had we lived in a more upscale neighborhood.

Nevertheless, due to a variety of factors, it was not unusual for the rich and the poor to live side-by-side in Korea, and robbers and other undesirables had more access to the homes of the rich than would have been the case if the rich had lived in the sort of gated communities now favored by the wealthy of those nations who have ready access to a wide range of consumer goods. The choicest houses were usually those with the readiest access to the tram, the markets, and other places of commerce and government.

Homemaking Chores in Korea

It should be remembered that during this time, there was relatively little in the way of modern appliances available. Cooking and heating, by and large, revolved around wood or coal stoves, which had to be prepared early in the morning and which required considerable maintenance for chopping wood, cleaning, stoking the fires, and so forth. Indoor plumbing was unknown — women had to walk several blocks or sometimes a mile or two within the city to obtain water, which was generally hauled back home in a jar on top of the woman's head. Almost every home had an outhouse and, in many cases, a garden into which the contents of the outhouse were periodically dumped as soil fertilizer. Food storage was sometimes a problem as well. Lacking modern refrigeration or even space for a pantry near the kitchen, we had to sometimes keep our food in less than optimal conditions. One spare bedroom was devoted to a food-storage pantry, mostly for potatoes. Sooner or later, the rats would get into the bedroom, and Youngchan and I would rid the bedroom of rats by chasing the rats into a large, brown, burlap bag that I would hold at the end of the potato pile while Youngchan would stir up the pile to remove the rats. After capturing the rats in the bag, I would slam the bag against the ground till all the rats were dead.

Homemaking chores occupied almost every Korean homemaker full-time and often required the assistance of other family members as well. Most homes in Korea were very simply made, being of cornstalk construction and covered over with lime and cement. They were wired for electricity in the city but had no indoor plumbing. Korean farmhouses are usually made with a plaster-over-chicken-wire construction and then whitewashed. A layer of dirt was supplied, and the outside dirt was used to raise pumpkins. The roofs of these farmhouses were usually thatched.

The dirt floors covered an ondahl — a series of pipes which spread the heat from the cooking fires into other rooms of the house. Persons entering the house were required to take their shoes off because the floor coverings of rice paper generally lasted several weeks before having to be replaced. Consequently the tasks of cleaning the floors and dusting did not occupy much time. However, emptying the contents of the outhouse into the garden, tending to the garden, fetching water, washing clothes by hand, caring for children, preparing food (including tofu, kimchee, mandoo, and other delicacies) required stamina and dedication. My father also was concerned that his family be well-fed. In addition to the vegetable garden that my grandparents helped to maintain, my father used to have a pomegranate tree in a three-foot in diameter pot. He would let it bloom outdoors during the summer. The plant would yield beautiful hibiscus-looking flowers until the end of June. (The plant would have been moved outdoors in the middle of March.) The plant would summer outdoors, producing fruit ready for eating in August. In October it would be moved back into the kitchen at the time of Chuseok.

Chickens were kept at most of the houses where we lived, especially after the family moved to the water-compound area. I was charged with keeping my father's chickens well-fed with grasshoppers and locusts. To obtain the insects, I generally frequented local farmland, foraging between the plants. In order to catch dragonflies, the most efficient way was to capture a female dragonfly and tie her tail to a stick that carried a quantity of cobwebs gleaned from the eaves beneath our farmhouse. Her sputtering in disgust at the whole proceeding would inevitably bring male dragonflies to the vicinity, who would attempt to mate with the hapless insect. My brother and I would capture the male dragonflies and put them into glass jars to be taken home and fed to the chickens. Sometimes when the supply of dragonflies ran low, Youngchan and I would go in search of frogs, whose legs would be chopped off to feed the chickens.

One day I found myself on a farm belonging to an ethnic Chinese family. One field was planted in soybeans, and after I had gathered my quota of insects, I and my friends decided to purloin a few soybean plants, figuring that the landowner would never miss a few soybean plants. Since soybeans are inedible raw, it was necessary to roast them over a fire in order to remove the water and make them crunchy. Unfortunately in the process of building a fire in a small pit, the landowner discovered me and my friends. Petty thievery and other mischief were typically handled on an individual, localized basis, and my friends and I were worried about what the landowner's punishment might be. I had heard of others being put into a brick oven in the field for a few hours in the heat of day as a punishment. Fortunately the landowner recognized me as the son of the man who had saved his life by taking him to the American missionary compound in Pyongyang. After a few, tense moments, the landowner told my friends and me to go home. I took care to avoid that particular field thereafter.

Laundry day generally involved washing all the clothes, both underwear and outerwear, by hand in a large tub using lye soap and hanging the clothes on a clothesline. For a family of two parents, four children, and two grandparents, this could be quite time-consuming and tedious. Of course we did not have so many clothes as people have nowadays, and we tended to wear them more than once during the week. Nevertheless, this chore could easily take most of the day and occupy more than one person.

One of our most time-consuming and thankless parts of this chore was washing Mother's silk gowns. To ensure that the silk would be free-flowing and unwrinkled, it was necessary to wash the silk dress by hand and then rinse it in fresh water containing a small amount of starch. The silk gown would then be wrapped around a three-inch in diameter oak-wood cylinder pole lying over a marble flat stone and then pounded with wooden hammer for two hours. The pounding would be accomplished over two to three days and usually involved my arm muscle pounding on the wooden cylinder pole with Youngchan pulling the fabric tight as I pounded. At the end of the pounding, my arms would be sore for a week! Although it would have seemed reasonable that an iron be used instead of pounding on the silk with a wooden hammer, the only iron available to us was one which had an internal compartment for hot coals. No electric iron was available or would have been allowed, inasmuch as ordinary civilians were not allowed to use electricity until evening when the few electrical appliances, such as electric lights, might be turned on.

With respect to clothes, I also helped my mother with making winter caps and mittens. Our family farm produced both wool and cotton, both of which I spun. The cotton thread spun was sold to cloth makers in the market, as was the wool yarn. Part of the wool yarn, however, was kept back to allow me to knit caps and mittens for the family against the harsh Korean winters.

Of course the most critical part of any homemaker's duties involves food preparation. I recall very well the frigid temperature inside the house in the early mornings of late fall and winter, as well as the significant efforts required of the adults in the household to prepare our meal. At dawn in the cold and crispy morning before sunrise, Grandmother, dressed loosely with her cotton-quilted shirt and skirt, came down to our dirt-floored kitchen. The kitchen was narrow enough to accommodate only two persons, as well as a firing platform into which were cemented cast-iron cooking pots of various sizes, usually twenty-eight, twenty and fifteen inches in diameter. As the kitchen was not heated during the night, the cold temperature of the kitchen caused Grandmother's breath to be visible every time she exhaled. She began by gathering an armful of kindling wood and wheat straw and quickly lighting a fire under two of the smaller-size cast-iron pots. When the fire was lit up fully, she added a bucketful of shiny coal pieces on top of the burning woodpile to make the fire hotter and last longer so that she could begin cooking and heating water. By this time, my father had entered the kitchen with a charcoal-burning hibachi and began preparing a hot fish soup side-by-side with Grandmother, who by then was busy cooking rice. The fish soup was prepared in a four-quart aluminum pan and placed over the hibachi.

To make the fish soup, Father defrosted a half dozen frozen haddocks and began slicing them in one- to two-inch pieces. He then added bite-sized sliced tofu pieces; a few stalks of napa cabbages; green-onion strips; a quarter-pound worth of thin, beef strips; a couple tablespoonfuls of hot bean paste diluted in two to three cups of water; and other seasoning powders. Usually it took about fifteen to twenty minutes of boiling the mixture in the pot before it was brought to the family table inside the main room. Because Korea is a peninsula, fish are relatively cheap in the local market. On the other hand, any meat substance, particularly beef, was unbelievably expensive, and an ordinary family could not afford to eat beef more than once per month or on a special occasion to entertain visiting relatives. Even then only a pound or less of beef was consumed by the entire family at any one time. Such a scarcity of beef was not due to a poor family budget, but it was more related to the availability of cattle. Most cattle were used for cultivating farmland or hauling heavy loads, and the only beef available in the market was meat of old and weak cows. Cattle raised for human consumption were practically unheard of. Consequently Koreans do not typically use oil or fatty foods (butter, cream) when cooking. Melting a little pork fat in the skillet, in which to fry vegetables or mung-bean pancakes, was the norm.

My hometown in Korea in winter had nearly subzero temperatures most of the four months of winter, and commonly the families had breakfasts with hot soups of vegetables, tofu , and haddock or beef so that their children particularly could hold some heat within their bodies while they walked 2 to 3½ miles to school. By the time we reached halfway to school, our scarves were covered with small icicles around our mouths and frost over our eyelashes. During my childhood, Koreans customarily had the best part of their daily meals at breakfast so that they could study or work at full strength during the entire day.

Each morning I washed my face in a pail of water, brushed my teeth with less than a half-palm-full of salt, and gathered my books in a cotton sack. Then as part of my routine chores, I lit another hibachi with charcoal and started boiling herbs and plant roots in a 1½- quart size ceramic pot. The herbs were given by my grandfather, who was a practitioner of ancient Chinese medicine, as medicine for Mother, who was suffering a long, protracted illness. Upon completion of a lengthy boiling process, all ingredients were filtered through a handkerchief-sized grass cloth, which was placed over the mouth of a teapot. Then the grass cloth was wrapped around the plant roots, and the dark-brown liquid was squeezed out to the last drop into the teapot and the solids discarded. Later in the morning, Grandmother or other members of the family offered Mother a cup or two of the liquid medicine I prepared. Despite the bitter-tasting medicine, my mother eventually died after about a year and a half from the onset of her illness.

By 6:30, the breakfast was placed on the dining table, which sat on the shiny ondahl floor. Our entire family, except Mother, who was ill in bed, gathered around the table. The table itself was of long, low construction, standing only a foot off the floor. It was made of either maple or birch wood, decorated by embedded bits of mother-of-pearl, and finished with black lacquer. The warm breakfast was complemented by the heat which rose from the ondahl floor, which was heated from the channels routed beneath the thick, limestone floor, utilizing the hot air resulting from the wood or coal flames used for cooking. After a long, chilly night of sleeping in a quilted-cotton mattress with my younger brother, it was good to sit on the warm floor and eat the warm soup with rice or barley. (Because the Japanese viceroy who occupied Korea prohibited Koreans from eating the pure and tasty short grain white rice during my childhood, we had to substitute the white rice mixed with other less tasty long grain rice or cheap, yellow rice or barley, which was considered highly undesirable. In those days, much of the white rice which was harvested in Korea was transported to the Japanese homeland or to their troops fighting overseas.)

At the breakfast table, occasionally my immediate brother picked out the best parts of the soup, such as the beef strips, before anyone else could get to it. I then gave him a small lecture with a hostile voice, "Be considerate to others and do not act like a pig by eating so much meat!" My father then slapped gently the top of my head and shouted at me, "Remember the rule: No one is allowed to talk at this breakfast table!" It was a Korean custom in those days that families took their meals without making conversation. If anyone talked during mealtime, it was considered unmannered, especially by the male members of the family, who were expected to refrain from unnecessary speech at all times. Men, especially fathers of some social standing, were typically laconic in speech. A traditional saying was that "men who speak more than five words per day are unstable."

At the end of breakfast, usually around seven o'clock, my younger brother and I packed our lunch boxes inside the sack of books and held them in our forearms and greeted our father with bowed heads as we left the front door. "Our respectable father, we, the humble children, wish to say good-bye, and we sincerely hope you have a great day, sir." We then headed toward school with the mercilessly cold Siberian wind whipping at our cheeks, which felt as if they had been sliced with sharp knives, both right and left.

Hazards of Walking to School

Walking to school during the extreme cold of winter was sometimes a very great trial.

As there were no school buses which picked up kids for school, it was necessary for us kids (myself, Youngchan, Heechan, and Inchon) to walk a fairly long way to school each morning, usually between 3½ to 5 miles one way. Father's access to a tram to take him to work figured prominently into his choice of houses to purchase and renovate as well.

Walks to school offered good exercise, although sometimes it was unpleasant if the day was especially cold or hot or if one met with unpleasant people or animals along the way. One hazard which was always present was the threat of a mean dog. Although most people kept their dogs leashed or chained to a pole outside the house, occasionally one would get loose and begin menacing passersby. In Korea most dogs were kept outside at all times, winter and summer, and lived in doghouses. They tended to be fierce creatures that were trained as watchdogs and were not the friendly house pets of my American experience. Consequently they tended to bite more readily. People often make fun of the old saying "the hair of the dog that bit me," especially when referring to a hangover. However, in Korea hair of the dog was often used, literally, as a remedy for dog bites. As a child, when I tried to play with various dogs, I would occasionally get bitten — sometimes lightly, sometimes hard. Then, as now, there was a fear of rabies from dog bites, although I had never heard of anyone getting their dogs vaccinated. And I had never heard of anyone taking rabies shots after getting bitten. The state of medicine at that time and place was such that home remedies were greatly relied upon. When I was bitten, especially if the bite was severe, Mother would confine my activities to the inside of a territory surrounded by water and not allow me to go near a deep lake or running stream or water. Mother believed that rabies, or hydrophobia, would induce me to run headlong into the body of water, possibly drowning myself. If the bite were less severe, Mother would request a piece of the dog hair, burn it over a candle, and apply it over the bite location. Severe bites would require the destruction of the dog.

Walking to school, I also had occasion to pass both a police station and a penitentiary.

As there was little access to individual means of transportation, including police transportation, there were more police stations located throughout Pyongyang than would probably be true for a city of comparable size in the U.S., simply because of the availability of police cars in the U.S. Being within ready reach of the police station afforded a measure of protection and was desirable from the homeowner's point of view in that home invasions were probably at least as prominent in Pyongyang during my childhood as is now true in certain of the tougher sections of some large U.S. cities. Koreans tend to be very jealous people, and those who had recently come into a large sum of money, such as lottery winners, were often at great risk of their lives, as most people kept their money at home hidden in a mattress, under a floor board, or in some unlikely looking place.

The police station was a rather fearsome place, even under the Japanese, who by my reckoning were more humane and gentler than the much fiercer Korean police. The police stations were responsible to the governors of the thirteen provinces (who, in most cases, were Japanese nationals). Nevertheless, aided by a system of informers on every block, the police, who were approximately 60 percent Japanese and 40 percent Korean, would conduct occasional forays into the houses of known or suspected criminals or rebels against the government. The unfortunate suspects would be hauled off to jail, where confessions would be extracted by any means necessary, including torture. Passing the police station, I was in a position to see through the basement window the torture of prisoners using the water-torture method (e.g., pouring water over the nose and mouth until the prisoner's belly swelled up and pressure would be applied to force the water back up through the esophagus and through the mouth or nose). I also saw the police beating the prisoners with bamboo canes. Although I saw several of these torture sessions, I never learned the identity of the prisoner, whether it was a common criminal (i.e., a suspect in a murder, robbery, or rape case) or a political prisoner. There was not much legal representation available in Korea in those days, and most of the judges were Japanese. Consequently the conviction rate for alleged felons in those days was fairly high, and the chances of avoiding prison were fairly low unless some sort of bribe could be arranged.

After conviction the prisoners would generally be sent to the penitentiary near my home, being transported in a paddy wagon with their faces covered by a bamboo hood. They would be required to wear a Japanese kimono colored in a bright, orangeish pink with thin socks and grass shoes. In those days, prisoners had to choose whether they would prefer to work outdoors (generally as part of the brick-manufacturing enterprise) or indoors (usually as part of the clothing-manufacturing enterprise). As previously related, my mother would usually buy our school clothes at the penitentiary when they had open-house public sales. The clothes would generally be very well made at a fairly low cost and last sufficiently well to be passed down to younger members of the family. Most prisoners, however, preferred to work outdoors making bricks, as it enabled them to view their surroundings and be in the open air. Their barracks, which contained a pit for their excrement, was enclosed and usually stank horrifically. Being in the open air was the only way to avoid the noxious smell. If a prisoner had put forth a good day's work, he would be allowed to run naked from the barracks to the shower building. If his work had not been satisfactory, he would be beaten soundly by the guards, who were often the Japanese or Korean police. Nourishment in the penitentiary was scanty; there was little food apart from rice and soybeans. And in Korea's severe climate, even the padded, pink kimonos did not afford much protection against the harsh winds and low temperatures, and the summer heat could prove almost unbearable. I often saw dead prisoners being wheeled out on a cart with their bodies covered with a sheet and their feet sticking out, having died either from the beatings, exposure to extreme temperature, or malnourishment. There was not much chance to escape from the penitentiary or from any other prison camp run by the Japanese, although some political prisoners did manage to do so eventually. Most of those who escaped went to Russia, where they trained as guerrilla fighters. They would then be sent back to Manchuria or North Korea, where they would make periodic forays into the rest of Korea unless captured by the Japanese. Political prisoners sometimes communicated on sheets using milk as a form of invisible ink. One of them (probably the original Kim Il-Sung) was released after playing crazy and eating his own excrement.

Several times when I was walking along the road past the prison on my way to the Japanese middle school, I saw throngs of black crows clustered in the poplar trees near the school. The crows, almost as large as ravens, made horrific noises, perhaps because there was little to eat in the vicinity. When I mentioned the crows to my grandparents, they looked very worried. They told me that the swarms of crows, particularly near the Japanese school, indicated that war was on its way, probably involving the Japanese.

Despite my pressures of school and work and helping my mother take care of the house, Father's garden, and the henhouse (or perhaps because of them), I occasionally descended into mischief. My house was close to a Buddhist monastery. The monastery, as a service to the community, rang a huge gong near its front door twice a day: once at midday, and the other time at 6 P.M. One day I thought it would be great fun to ring the gong early to confuse the populace. Just as I was preparing to ring the gong, however, a monk spotted me, shouted, and ran after me. I had to scramble quickly over the stone fence topped with barbed wire. My wrists still bear the scars from the barbed wire.

My maternal grandfather was a believer in traditional medicine, to the extent that he would make a special concoction of a venomous snake inside a bottle of sake. Supposedly the combination of the sake, the venomous serpent put alive into the sake, and the placement of the bottle containing the squirming snake into the ground for up to *three* years guaranteed a health elixir which was unsurpassed. People who were feeling unwell for whatever reason were often encouraged to drink small quantities of this strange brew to recover their health.

I had seen the bottle with the snake in it while I was still in fourth grade. My grandfather, as a rule, kept the bottle safely underground, but at one point I had been encouraged to drink a small quantity as a tonic. The elixir was strong and pungent but not unpleasant. The appearance of the dead serpent within the bottle, however, caused an unholy fascination. I wondered what reaction people would have if they saw the dead snake lying on the ground. One day, consumed with boredom and curiosity, I decided to find out. Removing the bottle from the lightly tamped hole in the dirt where it was customarily kept, I emptied the contents of the bottle on my neighbor's front lawn. It was not long till I heard my next-door neighbor, a young woman in an advanced stage of pregnancy, scream from her front yard. Startled by the appearance of the snake and not initially realizing it was dead, she had experienced a severe fright. When she came next door to my house, I denied all knowledge of it. However, when my father discovered the bottle missing from its normal location in its hole in the yard, he knew immediately what had happened and swatted my legs and behind severely until I confessed.

I was forced to appear in tears before his neighbor, who had at first been irate and in fear of losing her unborn child. Seeing my sincere repentance, however, she relented and assured my father that the only compensation she desired was for me to tutor her young daughter in math, which she was failing badly. To my credit, I was able to successfully tutor my neighbor's daughter so that she was able to pass her classes. Thereafter, I gave wide berth to my grandfather's traditional medicines unless specifically dosed with them by my grandmother!

On my way home from school, I would sometimes stop by my paternal grandparents' home to see if there was any way I could be of assistance to them. After their son's marriage, they had left the farm, which had provided at best a subsistence living, and had come to Pyongyang to live. My grandfather had set up small business selling water to the local women who had no indoor running water and who lived too far from any other city water tap to retrieve it comfortably. They would transport the water in jars poised on their heads back to their homes, sometimes in jars which would contain several gallons. As a separate sideline, my grandfather and grandmother opened their home as sort of a lodging house, which sold drinks and an occasional bed to laborers and porters who were engaged in manual labor. They would be sold drinks (usually sake or a creamy rice beer called shoju), as well as appetizers — usually soybean pancakes made with kimchi. I would often help my grandmother pulverize the soybeans and cook them into a mush. The mush would then be combined with kimchi and fried like ordinary pancakes. Although my grandparents were able to eke out a small living by this means, their clientele often did not pay directly and would be two to three months in arrears, meaning that their finances were always precarious. Nevertheless, they were able to maintain their independence until my father was able to finally move to the city-water-compound area, where there was sufficient room for them as well as for us, and were able to add to the family finances by means of tending a large garden.

Elementary School during the Japanese Era (1937–1945)

My father and mother both believed strongly in the value of an education, despite the fact that neither one of them had had the opportunity to go to college and the fact that my mother only had a sixth grade education. Therefore, it was not surprising that my father attempted to enroll me in a private, Presbyterian missionary school a year earlier than I would have been permitted to attend public school. Father wanted to encourage contact with the Americans, who he believed were a great nation with immense potential. He greatly respected the learning of the Protestant missionaries and wanted to ensure that I had sufficient exposure to the scientific method to permit later life improvement. He often mentioned that someday he hoped I would go to America to live and work. Nevertheless, the effort to provide a head start on my schooling was spectacularly unsuccessful. However learned the headmaster of the Presbyterian school might have been, he was a bit of a sadist and took undisguised pleasure in hitting those children who were unruly, disrespectful, or slow learners, especially if they were Koreans. As I had some language difficulties with English, I fell into the latter category at times and received more than my fair share of beatings. Things finally came to a head when one Sunday I elected not to attend church services and was soundly thrashed with a bamboo cane across the legs by the Presbyterian minister as a result. When my father saw the marks on my legs, he asked what I had done to earn it. I replied that I had not attended church on Sunday as the school required. Father said that he would attend the next Sunday's services with me to determine what Christianity was all about and work out the issue with the minister. True to his word, we both attended the next Sunday's services, and Father came away with a determination not to subject his eldest son to any more of that particular doctrine. He pulled me out of school and let me spend the rest of my year prior to enrollment in public school at home. To me this was no great hardship, as it permitted me to spend more time with my grandfather learning the one thousand Chinese characters, which all children were expected to know and recognize prior to entering Japanese school in those days. Also as private schools were viewed as being inferior to the public schools, it did not hurt my chances for educational advancement.

My religious education, as received from both school and family, emphasized kindness to others, as well as gratefulness for my life and society. About 3 percent of Koreans were Buddhist, 1½ percent were Christian, and the rest subscribed to Confucian philosophy, which although it does not emphasize a personal relationship with God, sets the cornerstone for ethical behavior in most parts of the Orient. The Japanese introduced Shintoism. Koreans were encouraged to worship at a Shinto shrine, where various Japanese gods were worshipped — usually past emperors and their families and aristocrats. Also worshipped were those who served the country in some way or who had died in a war for the country. Once every two months, the public-school kids would make official visits to the shrine and worship the gods there, marching in formation from the school to the shrine. The shrine (Jin Ja) built in Pyongyang had about three hundred limestone steps to climb. Schoolkids lined up at the base of the shrine and waited for their turn to climb up with their teachers. During WWII my father installed a miniature, wooden Shinto shrine in his house and made his two older kids pray each morning. Once every two months during the warm season on a Saturday morning, the entire student body and teachers would line up on the school playground to pay their respects to the soldiers who were once stationed in Pyongyang and who died on China's battleground. The bones and remains of each dead soldier were placed in a small (about fifteen inches), cubical, wooden box wrapped around with a white sheet and placed on a table with flowers. Usually a Japanese priest from a local Buddhist shrine conducted the ceremony.

It should be emphasized that the Japanese administration viewed school as being the ideal vehicle for assimilating the Koreans into the Japanese identity. As stated previously, each Korean child was expected to know and recognize one thousand Chinese characters ("kanji") prior to entrance into elementary school. Fluency in Chinese characters was taught via a poem entitled "The Thousand Character Essay," which contained the thousand Chinese characters. The poem, commissioned by Emperor Wu of the Liang Dynasty to Zhou Xingsi, was for his son to practice calligraphy. It was sung, much as Western children sing their own alphabet song, in order to help the children memorize the characters. Such mastery would permit the average person to comfortably read a Japanese newspaper. Learning the thousand Chinese characters was intended to facilitate the teaching of the Japanese language, which uses Chinese characters as part of its script. As Korea was viewed as a part of Japan, Japanese language and written script were considered to be the norm at school. However, due to the fact that many of the children came from families where Japanese was unknown prior to the annexation of Korea in 1910, during the first two years of school, a limited amount of hangul (Korean script) and Korean language was permitted, until such time as fluency in Japanese language and script could be achieved. It is worth noting that Chinese characters formed the basis of official government script for many years prior to the entrance of the Japanese into Korea despite the fact that King Yi had originated hangul several centuries prior to the 1900s. Hangul had been viewed as the language of women and the uneducated masses who were not clever enough to learn Chinese script, in which most of the classical literature of both China and Korea had been written and in which the business of government had continued to be conducted. Chinese script had thus provided a common written language among China, Japan, and Korea, though the pronunciation of the respective characters often differed greatly among the three nations. One feature of Oriental writing is that a Chinese word — for example, the word "I" — would be written in an elaborate manner and have a multisyllabic pronunciation in the Chinese language (Korean or Japanese) and use that language's pronunciation in place of the multisyllabic Chinese word. In a *Wall Street Journal* article of September 11, 2009, "To Save Its Dying Tongue, Indonesian Isle Orders Out for Korean," a discussion is provided about a schoolteacher in the Indonesian island of Buton (named Abidin) who is attempting to render the Cia-Cia language into Hangul in order to preserve it.

Other languages where this has been attempted has been for languages spoken in Nepal, as well as Lahu, a language spoken in China and Southeast Asia.

Also there are variations in the types of word usage, depending on the persons being addressed, and the situation in which the exchange takes place.

An example of high-class vs. low-class words includes the word for the head (mori) vs. the term for the low-class term for the heads of animals or children or low-class people, "tae-Gashi."

Similarly the polite term for eyes is "nun"; the low-class term is "nookkal." "Kumdoy" (black dog) is comparable to the Japanese "komduni (Negroes)". Bari — split foot (e.g., "cow" to represent the split foot resulting from the Japanese socks with a pocket for the large toe.) Westerners were referred to as "oranke" (yellow monkey). Yuan-fen means destiny or karma.

At one point, the Japanese had tried to obtain ownership of all the little islands just short of Kyushu, the southernmost Japanese main island. One of those islands, Okinawa gains its name from two Japanese words. The first, "oki," means "pond" while the word "na" means straw rope. The Japanese at one point considered linking all these islands, including the Truk islands (obtained as part of a German peace settlement after WWI) with straw rope. Enclosing this large area would increase the size of the empire.

There are rocks in the ocean that were tied together by huge ropes at least three inches in diameter. This was at Sedonaikai (a region of Japan).

"Tokyo" in kanji means "eastern castle." Nanking means "southern palace," Peking means "northern palace," and Shanghai means "palace arising from the sea." Seoul was Kyong-san. These names meant "elegant palace." Pyongyang, by contrast, was called "Heijo" in Japanese, meaning "flat land." Koreans called the city Piang. The Japanese homeland was "Nippon," meaning "origin of the sun." Korea was "Chosun," meaning "land of the morning calm."

Korean Classroom Orientation

Korean and Japanese students were segregated until middle school (grades seven through ten), at which point certain middle schools permitted a limited amount of integration depending upon the focus of the middle school. Also coeducation between boys and girls classes was unknown throughout all grades until the arrival of the Communist system due to the Confucian edict that "boys and girls shall not sit together past the age of six years old."

Schools during the Japanese era were run on a quasi-military basis. The principal of the school and his teachers expected to have blind obedience from the children or else there was always threat of a bamboo swat against the legs or a discussion with the child's parents, which would usually result in even more severe punishment. Although the elementary school did not have older students enforcing the school rules on behalf of the teachers, younger students were expected to look up to older students, who in turn would try to help the younger students with their studies. Additionally the normal school day would begin on the playground in a morning assembly meeting with a lecture by the principal or assistant principal. No coats, earmuffs, scarves, or hats were allowed, and sometimes frostbite occurred.

At each morning mass on the school playground, regardless of weather, students lined up like a checkerboard and read out loud in front of principal:

1) We are the citizens of the great imperial Japan.
2) We will work together and be faithful to our emperor.
3) We will be perseverant to any kind of hardship and show our thankfulness.

The meeting would begin with a listing of student misbehavior of those students who had been arrested or detained, as well as a listing of upcoming events.

At special occasions or national holidays, Emperor Hirohito in Tokyo sometimes delivered his speech (usually two hundred to three hundred words), and the students above fifth grade were expected to memorize his speech word by word within a week. Often the principal would say to the students, "You are the shoulders and right arms of future Japan. The future is yours. No matter what happens, you must study hard and grow up to be leaders and the backbone of our Great Japan!"

Also there would usually be an exercise session led by the athletic director with his commands broadcast over the loudspeaker. Students would have perhaps a minute to spread themselves out in a checkerboard fashion, maintaining a distance of about six feet apart, or as long as their arms would stretch. The loudspeaker provided a musical rhythm to synchronize the exercise. Exercises were oriented to grade level, with the most complicated exercises and steps being reserved for fifth and sixth grades. As part of our exercise training, we were taught the proper conduct to be followed during air raids. We were taught to lock arms to prevent one another from falling down and stampeding and to put out fires in the event of air raids and to pass buckets of water, fire-brigade style.

Third grade and above would have to align footsteps in the marching pattern. If the footsteps were not aligned, the teacher would make the kids repeat the marching pattern until the footsteps were aligned. Once the students were back in the classroom, shoes would be removed and put into a shoebox. Sometimes my shoes were stolen, and I would have to walk home without shoes.

Once the exercise session was over, the kids would march back to class. On our way to class, we would have to pass the portraits of famous men whom the Japanese taught us to admire. Abraham Lincoln and Napoleon Bonaparte were hanging on the wall, as well as others of Asian descent. As best as I can recall, the following were the men whose pictures were most prominently displayed:

1) Admiral Hideyoshi Togo. He won a huge naval battle with the Russians in the Sea of Japan although he lost many men in naval exercises prior to the battle. He knew there was quite a contingent of ships being sent from the Black Sea. He led war games in order to be ready for these ships. He trained his navy very severely, such that his ships collided with one another, and he lost a great many ships in that manner. The technology had been brought from Germany in large measure, and the Japanese trained their navy much as the German navy was trained. Although there was a question as to whether the ships were to come to Vladivostok or Kiyushu, between Korea and Japan in the Sea of Japan, they assumed that they would come through the Sea of Japan. Admiral Togo sank over thirty battleships from Russia, also winning Manchuria for a time (approximately 1910).

2) General Nogi. He was an army general who fought in Manchuria against the Russians (1910). After a great honor that celebrated the victory of the Japanese over the Russians in Manchuria (which utilized Molotov cocktails against tanks), General Nogi cut off his hair and committed hara-kiri, despondent over the fact of losing so many men. When he had been a small child, his father had poured a bucket of

water over him when he resisted carrying water from the well to the house during a cold night. The purpose of pouring the bucket of water over him was to show him how much he needed to strengthen his body and mind in order to overcome any hardship.

3) Yi Su-zhin. A court noble who was prominent in the origin and preservation of Korean cultural and literary life. He lived about five hundred years ago. Someone had drawn a picture of him with a grass-cloth type of crown.

4) OishiYoishio. The master of the forty-seven samurai, who avenged their master's death on the Buddhist priest who had been the cause.

5) Nakano. A child who lived in a temple school and walked a great distance to take his mother medicine. He then walked back to the temple in a snowstorm.

6) Noguchi (Hideoshi). When he was a child, he accidentally burned his hand from a pot of soup. His hand became infected, and his fingers became stuck together, such that he could not open his hand at all. An American doctor treated his hand (this was during Meiji or Hirohito's time) and made him able to separate the fingers. Instead of practicing as a doctor to obtain lots of money, he went to South America to treat yellow fever victims. He died of yellow fever himself.

On arriving back in the classroom, the kids would sit quietly in their seats until the teacher arrived in class. The class leader would inform as to when the teacher arrived, when to bow, and when to sit. After the usual morning mass and beginning of the first class period, the students again started to read aloud:

1) Follow good ethics
2) Observe rules
3) Accomplish responsibility
4) Show thankfulness

The curriculum taught in elementary school included ethics, reading, math, history, geography, art, and black ink-brush writing. I spent a fair amount of time in Japanese school learning kanji, hiragana, katakana, and using a calligraphy brush. The ink for the brush was made by rubbing a black block (probably some form of carbon) against another stone to produce a black powder, which was then transferred to a small container of water nearby. The brushstrokes of the brush were deemed to make a person have a clear mind, inasmuch as intense concentration was required to produce the correct thickness of the character stroke, an integral part of the character formation and the readers' ability to decipher. The calligraphy lessons were typically given at long, low tables with large sheets of paper. Characters were drawn large to ensure that the proper letter and brush strokes were maintained. It should be observed that hiragana is a form of writing that is derived from kanji, much as cursive writing is derived from block letters in English.

The first class of every day was a class in ethics. Once every other week, the school principal would teach ethics from a textbook. Examples of old Japanese people who were dedicated to their masters or examples of exemplary service to others were provided in the textbook. Obedience to the government, parents, and others was strongly stressed, and the children were made to understand that they were expected to be good citizens of Japan. His lectures were referred to as "su-shin" or "soul polishing."

Reading classes were carried out in Japanese and typically included stories from a textbook that contained a variety of Japanese legends and stories.

Children were expected to have mastered the multiplication tables between one times one through nine times nine by the end of first grade. Mastery of the multiplication tables was facilitated by use of a mnemonic device, a sing-song chant that the children would sing during their classes.

History and geography lessons were carried out with the aid of maps, as well as Japanese history textbooks that detailed the history and culture of Japan. Korean textbooks were unknown in my school; indeed I later heard of Japanese book burnings of Korean history texts. We were taught that the Japanese empire was indeed our empire and that we belonged to it as fellow Japanese. We were taught the legend of the pigeon that descended on the bow of the first emperor, who was fighting other tribes of Japan. His name was Jing-Mu. The pigeon's rays shone forth from atop the bow and blinded the warriors of the other side. The name of the pigeon-goddess was Amateras (goddess) O-Mikami (who created Japan).[1,2]

Closely allied to the story of Amateras was another legend of the snake with eight heads and eight tails (Yamata no Orochi) who, when split open, was discovered to have both a mirror and a sword in its belly.[3] Although both items were handed down by the emperor's family, there have been suggestions, however, that while the mirror is located within the Ishi shrine, the sword is located at the Atsuta shrine in Nagoya, and the jewel is located in the Imperial Palace in Tokyo.

No knowledge of Korean history or language was allowed in any school. No mention was made of Tangun, the legendary (mythic) founder of Korea, whose father had supposedly descended from the heavens and mated with the bear-woman. All textbooks were in Japanese. All music lessons were taught using Japanese songs or themes from European classical music/operas. Likewise all art classes were taught in the style of European impressionism. Young children were taught early to draw and paint not only with an eye to Japanese culture, but in the impressionist style. It should be noted that most of the cultural features of these Japanese- Korean schools, including art, music, and drama, were based upon European cultural heritage. Very little in the way of Asian music or art found its way into the public schools, apart from children's songs or marching songs, as well as black ink-brush writing, which we were required to practice in order to perfect our mastery of the Chinese characters. Art especially was related to European impressionism, and traditional European operas were very popular. Background music in teahouses was largely opera. The Japanese neither encouraged nor discouraged the teaching of traditional songs and art. Sometimes there would be a musical contest between the schools. Schumann, Beethoven, and other European composers would be featured prominently. Such contests would normally be held on Sundays or other holidays. The reason for not teaching Korean traditional art and music was that the traditional art and music was considered to be too relaxed and not dynamic enough, unlike European art and music. Training in European classical music and arts was provided to educate students to encourage them to depart from their traditional "calm and quiet lifestyle" and adopt a more progressive and dynamic approach to life. The Russian educational system, which was introduced in 1945, thought the same way, taking pains to abolish Korean music and arts and substituting their own lively songs, music, and painting styles.

Despite the facts that Korean history and culture were no longer allowed to be taught in school and that Father worked for the Japanese-controlled city hall as manager of the water-meter design and testing laboratory (it was not easy for any Korean to be a manager in city hall or other governmental institute), I was able to sense his deep attachment to his native country. He seldom spoke of it, fearing the repercussions if Korean patriotism was shown to his children, who might mention it to their friends. He spoke to me about Korean history and patriotism when I was about fourteen years and older and made me realize my true heritage, despite the attempts of the Japanese viceroy to turn Korea into a Japanese colony. It was sometime during my third grade period that the Viceroy commanded all Koreans to change their names to Japanese names. Reluctantly most Koreans changed their names within a year. Thereafter my last name and first name became Muriyama and Masao, respectively. The Chinese characters for Rhee indicate a small boy standing under an apricot tree while the Chinese characters for Muriyama, which is three trees, means heavily forested mountain. Similarly the Korean name Kim, whose Chinese characters mean money, was changed to Kanezawa, which means pile of money.

Teachers would eat lunch with students. They would pray for soldiers prior to lunch, to which the students would respond: *idet e kamas* (I am very grateful for eating this food). No student would be allowed to eat Korean white rice; the Koreans had to eat Taiwanese rice or barley. One day the board of education inspected all the school lunches to ensure that none of the Korean kids had white rice in their lunches. Fortunately my teacher found out that I had white rice in my lunch before it was spotted by the board of education inspectors. He asked me to take the lunch box back home, which I did. However, my home was so far from the school, I barely made it back prior to the last class of the day.

Teachers would often trade classes if it involved subjects with which they were not comfortable. Often a female teacher would ask a male teacher to teach gym class, and often male teachers would ask female teachers to teach music classes. Art classes were often among those which would be traded off, as many teachers were not comfortable teaching art.

At 2:30 or 3:00, the school day would end, and the kids would help clean the school. Part of the school day would be devoted to sports (rugby, acrobatics, etc.). Gym classes were typically three to four hours per week, with basketball and soccer games being allowed if the students were not required to help clean the classrooms. Typically the students had to help clean classrooms twice a week.

Janitors cleaning the buildings were unknown. They were expected to repair the buildings and building equipment, not clean the rooms. The kids were expected to clean the rooms, which usually meant sweeping the rooms. Students were also expected to fuel and take care of the stoves, which were usually in the center of the classroom. The floors were wooden, and no one could wear shoes indoors, except teachers, who were allowed to wear slippers. Students sat two per desk. The floors never got really dirty, just a little dusty. Floors were mopped with water, moving the desks from side to side within the rooms. Students then waxed the floors with wax brought from home, sometimes with the ends of candlesticks, usually once a week. The class leader would request that the teacher come and inspect the job done. The teacher would inspect, often in the corners, and if not done appropriately, would ask that the job be redone. If the job needed to be redone two or three times, it would cause the students to have to come home very late, although the parents would not dare complain. If the teacher was too particular, he or she might find a spot on the floor that was highly polished, which would be slippery to their indoor slippers.

In elementary school and also in middle school, the upper classmen (fifth and sixth grade students) would be enlisted to help younger kids who were having trouble in school. During the graduation of the sixth grade pupils, the fifth grade girls would cry because they were losing their older (sixth grade) sisters. The younger girls would sing a farewell song that began, "We studied under the lightning bug, near the window with melting snow…" to the tune of "Auld Lang Syne," about the fact that all the hard work over the past few years had really paid off, but now the younger girls were losing their older sisters. Although most of the kids would not have the opportunity to go to middle school after elementary school, most of them went on to lead productive lives.

Elementary School Athletics

Physical activity was highly emphasized in all grades from elementary through middle school under the Japanese, the Russians, and the North Koreans. A strong body was especially desirable in light of the fact that so much manual work was required just to keep body and soul together and the fact that transportation options were limited, making it necessary to be able to walk long distances carrying heavy burdens. Additionally having a well-trained cadre of school children to impress visiting dignitaries with their athletic abilities and marching skills was something that all three regimes considered important. Fortunately students were allowed to play Korean games at the playground during off class periods, so the concept of fun was allowed to permeate all our intense physical, militaristic training.

The Japanese especially were very fond of field days where track and obstacle courses were run from first through sixth grades. In mid-August or the first part of September, the school organized a field day that lasted three or four days in a row. There would be tents set up for the parents to come watch their kids as they competed in various track events. High jump, broad jump, 100-meter race — all the typical track events were featured. The events often resembled triathlons in that the participants might start out in a race but have to negotiate an obstacle course or jump over obstacles or crawl under a large net spread over the ground with wooden rifles on their backs.

Our field-day activities included suicide-bombing tactics. The setup would be that three to four groups would oppose one another, with each group consisting of three to four students. The students together would carry a simulated bomb made out of wood or sheet metal. The bomb was about six to eight inches in diameter, thirty to forty feet long, and forty to fifty pounds. The purpose was to practice transporting the "bomb" to the enemy gate about seventy yards from the starting line. Whoever bumped the gate first was the winner. (There was no ordnance in the simulated bomb, of course.) The idea for this type of competition arose from the war with China, where the Japanese used similar tactics against Chinese fortifications in 1910. Japanese composers had written songs about the soldiers who had sacrificed their lives to deliver the suicide bombs at the time. Also there were tug-of-war games, which strengthened the arms and backs of all those involved. Another "game" type military tactic was to have one hundred students topple an opponent's pole. The strategy involved having two teams, with one pole for each team, with two regiments trying to knock down the opponent's pole. Each pole was thirty to thirty-five feet tall. The students would try to knock their opponent's pole down by either knocking down the students who were holding the pole or by climbing on the student's backs who were holding the pole, climbing the pole, and trying to drag the pole down. This game was simulated at the Japanese naval academy, and they were trying to encourage the kids to become fit enough physically to participate in this activity. My mother aggressively urged me to do well in the field day and reminded me before the day started, "Remember, son, you cannot be beaten by other kids!" If I did not win a major field-day event, she would shun me and make me feel very guilty.

During the holidays where track and field events would be exhibited, there would also be a display of marching prowess in competition with other schools in Pyongyang. This also was true for the three regimes, but especially under the Japanese regime, which expected that the marching demonstration mirror the marching exercises performed in the Japanese army. All the footsteps had to be matched throughout each class, from third through sixth grade students. The school reviewer (usually the school principal) would never provide many compliments — probably the best a particular class could hope for would be something along the lines of, "You all seem somewhat better than yesterday, but there is still a lot that needs to be improved. First of all, your footsteps were too weak. I did not hear the ground trembling. For a punishment, you are required to march another thirty minutes." Sometimes the children would fall to the ground, fainting from the heat, when required to do more marching. However, they would be permitted to lie there until they had recovered themselves. The school principal did not believe that his request for improved performance was unreasonable. On the contrary, it would make the students' bodies stronger and capable of greater feats of will and self-sacrifice in service to the government.

School Holidays

Most of the Korean school holidays were related in some manner to Japanese holidays. The Japanese, wanting to be Westernized insofar as their educational curricula were concerned, extended this desire for Westernization to the calendar. Gone were the holidays of lunar new year, as well as the Korean traditional agricultural festivals. Although lunar new year could be privately celebrated at home, no school holiday was provided for that day. Chusok, which is similar to the Japanese Bon holiday and commemorates the dead, occurs approximately one month after the Bon holiday and was the one holiday that the Koreans were permitted to openly celebrate and that allowed for time off from school, if required, to visit the graveyard of one's deceased ancestors.

Typically holidays were arranged such that at least one holiday occurred every month. For example, the New Year's celebration was considered of great importance and usually coincided with the last of the winter vacation, which lasted about a month. This was an opportunity for the kids to go ice skating on the Ta Dong river or to play games with a *jianzi,* which is more or less a beanbag that incorporates feathers and is used to test the player's agility in keeping it in the air.

February 10 (egenseitz) was celebrated as the creation day for Japan. Also it celebrated the victory of the very first Japanese emperor over the tribes of Japan. All the kids would get together and read solemnly a history of how Japan was created. This was one occasion on which a speech by Emperor Hirohito might be read by the school principal, very solemnly, in front of the students with bowed heads that could not be raised until the speech was over. Copies of the emperor's speeches were kept in a small shrine (fifteen feet by fifteen feet) next to his picture in a locked box twenty to thirty steps above the ground with nice landscaping around the shrine. The emperor was considered a "living god" who required a solemn aspect when being addressed, special language, and absolute obedience. His presumed divinity did not extend to imputing supernatural powers to him but rather recognition of the fact that he was considered to be descended from a deity and therefore worthy of veneration.

Emperor Hirohito's birthday was April 25, which typically was the day that the cherry blossoms would begin blooming. Kids would have the day off, and the city water commission would host a picnic with free lunches for the workers in the city water area next to the city park. At one of those picnics, my grandmother became drunk and began dancing in the street, which was politely disregarded by the police!

Emperor Meiji's birthday (Meiji-sitsu, October 3) was usually the day on which the chrysanthemums bloomed. Emperor Meiji was the grandfather of Emperor Hirohito and was the prominent force behind bringing back technological and medical knowledge from the outside world, mostly from Germany and the U.S. Although much of the knowledge his emissaries brought back was militaristic and enabled Japan to challenge the Russians and Chinese, they also brought back medical, scientific, artistic, and musical knowledge and contributed to making Japan a modern society.

The anniversary day of Japanese victory fighting in Manchuria against Russia in 1910 was celebrated during Armed Forces Day, which occurred sometime in May. There was an army compound inside Pyongyang that housed nearly one division of Japanese soldiers. Elementary school students were invited to spend one day at the army compound with the soldiers and watch their bayonet practice and demonstrations of other military weapons' capabilities. Students would tour the entire compound, including the soldiers' living quarters. Soldiers ate with kids at the same dining table for lunch and dinner. At the end of the day, students were given a small gift to take home.

On a few special occasions during the school year, such as the Provincial Board of Education visiting the school as part of a national holiday celebration, the upper-class students were required to participate in a parade at the city hall square in front of the dignitaries. From about two weeks prior to the parade, students, led by the teachers, practiced the parade by marching in front of the school principal and singing army war songs. The footsteps were required to line up like a stream of waves. If there was any dissatisfaction by the principal, students were forced to repeat the marching over and over several times during the afternoon. Sometimes the ground was so dusty that the students could not see more than twenty feet away. Occasionally kids collapsed to the ground from heat under intensive sun rays. At the end of rehearsal, the principal made his usual statement, "Well done, you students. I am pleased with your efforts and dedication to make the upcoming parade successful, but there is still something that needs to be improved…."

There were a variety of other small holidays, such as the girl's doll holiday, celebrated on March 3, and the boy's holiday celebrated on May 5. Although these holidays were celebrated at home, they were not school vacation days. Of course our birthdays were not considered school holidays; indeed they were rarely celebrated at all, not even at home, with a couple of exceptions. The first-hundred-days celebration for the baby was traditionally a celebration for the survival of the baby and the mother. Korean life was very hard, and there were a great number of miscarriages, early infant deaths, and maternal deaths in those days. Babies were often not named until they had survived one hundred days, and then the names would often be derived from the objects that the infant would grab for when placed on a table. Reaching for a pen or a book would often indicate a scribe; reaching for money would indicate a future successful merchant. Otherwise birthday celebrations were not a big deal, and birthday presents would be small and insignificant. The most I ever received for my birthday from my mother was fifteen zon (equivalent to about ten cents). I was told, "Today is your birthday. Here is fifteen zon. How about getting yourself a steamed flour cake from the Chinese restaurant?" I would walk to the restaurant, even when it was snowing, and bring home two buns filled with sweet, red bean filling — one for Mother and one for me.

There were a variety of irregular school holidays as well. We would have school field trips (sometimes as far away as Seoul), where we would view modern technological wonders, such as X-ray machines, and take factory tours. We would stay in a hotel overnight and sometimes have to confront the bad behavior of some of our classmates, who would begin behaving badly by making a mess at the table, putting bowls of rice on top of their heads, and so forth. Once I myself got into rather a spot of mischief by trying to cross a creek that was deeper than supposed. My teacher refused to help rescue me when he saw that I was floating down the stream. Fortunately I was able to grab onto a tree branch and climb out on my own.

Sometimes the teachers would arrange for the kids to have picnics in a park or in the mountains with each of us carrying our own food in our own knapsacks. Mothers would usually sew the knapsack from white cloth and pack seaweed rice along with a soft drink. Students would sing songs as they marched to the park. Parents might be invited to the picnic, although my parents did not usually attend even though my father was an important member of the PTA and contributed a lot of money to the school.

After the battles of Nanking and Shanghai, the class would also visit the city convention center, where the blood-soaked uniforms and bones of the Japanese soldiers who had been fighting in China would be displayed. We were expected to bow and pray in front of these displays in order to pay homage to the spirits of those soldiers who had died in battle. While viewing one of these displays, the school principal would read the Japanese emperor's speech, and the kids would sing the Japanese national anthem. "Japanese emperor's era should last till a small pebble grows up to be a large boulder." The text of the

Japanese emperor's speech was kept in a shrine and handled with great ceremony, with people bowing deeply to the text and handling it at arm's length. The Japanese emperor's speech was quite formal and different from the commoner's speech. The emperor himself was termed "kimi."

In addition to attending the exhibitions, there were plays, usually about once a year. In fourth grade, I was selected to play the role of a Japanese soldier carrying a bugle in his hand among twenty other students in the play, showing how an enemy castle would be attacked. These activities were intended to build patriotism towards the Japanese empire and to encourage the students to be part of the war against the rest of the world. The Japanese believed they would always being moving forward, and they wanted the Koreans to be part of the police force that would control the colonies. The audiences of the play were, for the most part, parents of the students, as well as Japanese wounded soldiers with crutches, their superiors, and some important figures of government institutions. When the play was over, my mother congratulated me for participating in the success of the play. This was the last time my mother ever attended any of my school events. Thereafter her health problems made it impossible for her to attend any school affair.

When I was a teenager during WWII, one of my tasks (imposed by my father) was participation in "neighbor watching," similar in some respects to "neighborhood watch" in the U.S., only there was more active participation by the watchers. During the time of the watch, I was expected to walk around the neighborhood for an hour, beginning at 11 P.M. for the first shift and 2 A.M. for the second shift. (Other boys would take earlier and later shifts.) Each boy would be led by an adult as the two of them would patrol the neighborhood, the boy clapping two pieces of oak together and shouting and singing at the top of his lungs. The idea was to frighten away or detect any thieves who might be lurking. The only weapon I ever carried was a Japanese wooden sword used in my martial arts class, but on which I was very proficient. Typically the watchers would perform one night and then be off for several nights. The number of houses watched was approximately fifty to one hundred, all side-by-side and very compact. Some kids would carry a gong and wake up the neighbors. None of this "watching" was paid; it was completely voluntary as part of living in the neighborhood. Another voluntary activity was the creation of fire brigades during the bombing attacks. When someone's house began to burn, neighbors would form a bucket line to pass buckets of water to help put out the fire.

As a biweekly school assignment, I was expected to write letters to the soldiers, who would usually respond, sometimes with sketches of the frontline or Chinese children with the Japanese flag. Additionally we were expected to send little gifts of soap and cigarettes to the soldiers. The items were collected from neighbors and sent via little, white bags called "eimom-bukuro." Korean women would also collect plus marks on a towel (needlework stitches in red over a white towel, usually at least a hundred plus marks per towel, to be tied to the soldier's head for good luck) from passersby. I would then put the towel into the bag with the soap and the cigarettes and send them to the soldiers or give them personally when we saw them off at the railroad station on their way to the frontlines. Most enlisted soldiers were quartered in cargo carriers with crowded, wooden bunkers and straw mattresses. They were glad to get off the train for thirty to forty minutes by the train track to breathe some fresh air and refresh themselves at the drinking-water fountains. Students lined up around the soldiers and waved handheld Japanese paper flags while singing the war-marching songs. Sometimes the soldiers handed out a few candy bars to the students to express thankfulness for seeing them off to the war.

Elementary School Health Issues

There were numerous diseases that ravaged the Korean population, especially its youngest members. Malaria, leprosy, tuberculosis, and other serious infectious diseases were quite common and had no preventive vaccines. Numerous environmental issues, such as bad water and daily contact with poisonous insects, snakes, and parasites (such as worms), preyed on the population, especially its poorer members. All elementary school children had checkups given by medical doctors at the school. Sometimes they would find worms in the stomach, usually contracted from eating raw vegetables. The kids would be given medicine to kill the worms, which would last for about two to three months, until the next exam period. Tuberculosis was also a disease that was prevalent with the students. Children who had tuberculosis would be asked to wear a mask in order to prevent transmission of the disease. Formation of scabs on top of a kid's head and suffering from trachoma eye disease were not uncommon among the schoolkids, and they were treated by the attending nurses at the school dispensary rooms. Malaria also sometimes occurred — once when I had a high fever from malaria, I cured myself by running vigorously until the fever broke. At PTA meetings, parents expressed their gratitude toward the city board of health for providing such routine medical examinations at school. Home health care for children was extremely expensive and difficult for most poor parents.

Bedbugs were also a nuisance in Korea while I was growing up. Legend had it that they had been imported from China in the pipe of a scholar who had found them interesting and planned to study them at length. He brought them in his pipe to smuggle them past the guards. Unfortunately some of them escaped his custody and began propagating themselves in bedclothes, pillows, and clothing. They were pervasive, annoying, and nearly impossible to get rid of. They would secrete themselves in furniture joints, in addition to the futons, bedclothes and clothing of everyday life. The bedclothes and clothing were washed in hot water, which stopped their propagation for a time, but they always came back. Their primary residence seemed to be in the furniture joints of our chest of drawers and tables. Once a year, usually in the spring, my father would assemble the furniture outside and douse it with gasoline. That worked temporarily, and we were relatively free of bedbugs for about a year.

Once when I was a small child, I tried to show how conscious of cleanliness I was by pouring gasoline over a portion of the floor where my father had been cutting hair, in order to sanitize the floor. Unfortunately I also tried to activate the electric hair clippers shortly thereafter, which caused an explosive fire. Fortunately my father was able to put out the fire with a futon.

My brother Youngchan and I were once in a position to assist my grandmother in avoiding being bitten by a centipede. Centipedes in Korea were large creatures (approximately four inches long) and poisonous. Hence when the centipede crawled down the back of grandmother's dress, we lost no time in helping her remove it from her clothes.

Centipedes were sometimes used in folk medicine, i.e., made into a tincture with alcohol. Several live centipedes would be put into a bottle of alcohol until their juices had been sufficiently imparted to the liquid, usually a matter of a month or more. Then the resulting liquid would be fed in a spoon to a patient looking for relief of some ailment or another. Centipedes were usually fairly easy to capture; as a rule, all that was required was to place a hunk of cooked chicken into the cellar or wherever centipedes were thought to be located. Usually by the next day, there would be several large specimens clinging to the meat and ready to go into the alcohol bottle.

The recourse of traditional Korean medicine went beyond centipede tinctures, however. As a rather sickly child, I can remember clearly the day my mother took me to my grandfather's house to receive an acupuncture treatment for jaundice and fever. I was only five years old and was not prepared for what was about to happen. With a stainless steel, approximately 1.5 mm diameter needle, he pierced my back (near the spine) in three different locations and covered the pierced holes with a suction jar that had a burning cotton rag soaked with alcohol. It hurt, and I could hardly bear the pain on my back. As soon as the suction cup was placed on my back, I started to run away from him, and I hid inside his flower garden. I ducked my head below the tip of the flower stem so that he would not find me. The suction cup was still attached to my back. Suddenly I got a bee sting on my thumb. I was suffering from the bee sting more than the acupuncture treatment. I started to yell, "MOM." The first words I heard were, "There he is," and she replied, "Why are you still shouting? Keep your voice down and come into the house!" When she discovered that I was shouting because of the bee sting, grandfather approached slowly and said, "See what you get for running away from me!" He pulled out the bee's black stinger from my thumb and wrapped my thumb with soybean paste. I asked, "What about the suction cup on my back?" He answered "That will stay with you for the rest of your life. Ho! Ho!" And he laughed. By then I started to have tears running down my face. Mother asked Grandfather, "Please do something for the suffering child." By that time, the suction cup fell off by itself from my back, losing the intensity of the vacuum within the jar. I thought I was released from all the suffering then and made up my mind not to go to Grandfather's house again with mother without knowing what he was up to. About ten days later, the color of my skin improved, the occasional fever was gone, and the diarrhea also stopped. At the end of a month and a half or so, my skin color became completely normal. After all, I was glad that Grandfather did what he could to treat me.

Another time I fell into the sewage canal, which varied from three- to six-feet wide, that surrounded the school. The sewage canal was the place where manure was sold by people whose job it was to clean out the latrines of the Korean household. They generally deposited the manure at the edge of one of the Korean rivers that ran through Pyongyang. Farmers wishing to purchase the manure could do so next to the sewage canal.

I attempted to jump across it on a dare from some classmates who had threatened to beat me up unless I did so. I swallowed some of the canal water and had to be given artificial resuscitation by some of the teachers. I spent ten days in the hospital, and the kids who had threatened me into trying to jump across the canal were suspended from school for two weeks.

When I was very young (1½ to 3 years old), my father gave me wild ginseng root together with watermelon when I became very ill with an infection that caused severe jaundice. I gradually recovered from this illness despite having nearly died. The wild ginseng root has tremendous healing properties, something which modern society is just beginning to appreciate. The Russians searched for it immediately upon entering Korea, disdaining the farmed ginseng root, which was much less powerful. Some wild ginseng root was given to Stalin, but before it could really take effect, he was murdered.

Another time when I was very young, I had a serious head injury due to the fact that I was playing with my father's pocketknife, which had been left on top of the dresser. Unfortunately I dropped the knife and jumped down on a pile of quilts more or less simultaneously, which led to my head being cut open with the knife and losing a lot of blood. Although my mother tried to stanch the flow of blood using tobacco, that remedy only temporarily stopped the bleeding. It was left to my father to carry me to a local Japanese doctor, who stitched up the cut. The doctor cautioned my father that I had lost a lot of blood, and he (the doctor) could not promise that I would live. The doctor did the best he could, however, bandaging the head all around and even wrapping bandages underneath the chin. My father picked me up and cradled me tenderly, even having a picture taken in that pose: a small, bandaged boy being held close to his father's chest. That was a very unusual display of affection in an otherwise rigid society.

Recreation outside of Elementary School

One of my fondest early childhood memories is the time when my father took the entire family to an evening bazaar with vendors sitting under their tents selling their wares and using gas lamps for illumination in the early evening hours. My father bought very little except for a large watermelon, which he brought home and put in a tub of water to keep cool for the family to eat the next day.

However, our weekends and after-school hours were not really free. Not only were we expected to do homework during this time, we also spent half a day each Saturday cleaning up trash (including cigarette butts) in the city's public facilities. Sundays were usually spent going with our teacher to the movies for free, the expenses being paid by the school administration. Only movies approved by the school administration and the state were allowed and typically involved heroic battles in war movies of soldiers fighting in China or the stories of Japanese heroes who were loyal to Japan and the emperor. However, there was one samurai movie with a love story subplot that captured my fancy. I was able to sneak in with one of my friends to see this movie but was spotted by a couple of teachers who had been given free passes just to ensure that they could capture students who were going to unapproved movies. Fortunately I overheard the teacher's comments about the fact that they had spotted the "little kids" and managed to get out of the theatre and run home prior to being caught by the teachers. As one got older, there was much more freedom of choice as to which movies one could watch.

One of the few nonmilitary movies that I was allowed to watch when I was in elementary school was *Shi-Bu-Wang*. Shi-Bu-Wang is the guardian spirit of the underworld, the being who is responsible for the final destination of deceased spirits. His name translates to Earth-Father-God.

The movie *Shi-Bu-Wang* was displayed by an independent Korean theatre owner who was unconnected with the major theatres of Pyongyang. My uncle Yu took me to see the movie. I had asked Uncle Yu to take me, as I was afraid to ask Father. Father disapproved of all movie-going on the basis that it took time away from my studies. Additionally the Japanese administration did not approve of movies containing love stories and maintained a list of prohibited movies. Students caught viewing a prohibited movie were subject to censure or expulsion. Although we believed that *Shi-Bu-Wang* was not on the prohibited-movies list, one could never be certain.

As I entered the theatre, there was a large movie poster for *Shi-Bu-Wang*. It depicted a man hung from a tree with a bleeding chest and bleeding mouth. Uncle Yu bought the tickets as we entered the theatre.

The movie had to do with life immediately after death and showed a person as he descended through the various circles of Hell. Upon arrival at the first gate, Shi-Bu-Wang or his assistant reviewed the life of the deceased, checking first to verify if the date of death was correct. If the person had arrived too soon, he was sent back to earth (probably undergoing a near-death experience). A book containing the history of the person's deeds on Earth was reviewed by several beings, who searched for mention of the person's misdeeds. If the person was a good person with only minor failings, he was directed on the stairway that led to Heaven. If he were a person with many sins recorded, his sins would be punished sequentially, in order of their magnitude, until his soul was finally cast into the black pit of Hell. If a person had told many lies, he was taken to a room where his tongue would be torn out. If he had been unkind to wild animals, he would be transformed into a wild animal and sent back to earth, where he would experience the human cruelties involved in hunting, trapping, and slaughter. If he had been a thief, he would have his hand cut off by a machine. If he had been an adulterer, he would be ushered into a room with a bed of nails and forced to roll about the bed until his back was bloody and he screamed for mercy. After all the appropriate punishments were indicated by the red tags on the unfortunate's shirt, the person would be cast into Hell, never to be seen or heard from again. I do not remember what happened in the case of an ordinary, decent person with a few transgressions in his past. Presumably if the person's good deeds far outweighed his bad deeds, he would be sent to Heaven after a suitable period of punishment. The movie was something of a revelation for a fourth grader, and I experienced nightmares about it long thereafter. It certainly colored my thinking about the afterlife!

In addition to the movies, we were allowed to visit an occasional museum, such as the one near Moran-bong where my Uncle Zon (Mother's half sister's husband) worked as a guard and overseer of the museum activities and caretaker of its treasures. The museum was run by the institute of the Pyong-an-Namdo province and administered by Japanese staff personnel. About one-half of the total employees were Koreans — Uncle Zon was one of them. He had been born and reared in a farming family on the southern tip of the Korean peninsula named Zol-la Namdo. He spoke with a heavy southern accent, and it created some difficulty communicating with us. Fortunately he spoke fluent

Japanese and was able to communicate with me and my immediate brother in Japanese most of the time. Having been a farmer in his early life, he was very muscular. Although his was a background of little culture and education, Uncle Zon had obtained an education in archaeology at a Japanese school as well as an interest in Far Eastern history. He was well-suited for working in the museum as a security guard. Furthermore since my father was a staff member of Heijo City Hall, his recommendation for my uncle was well-accepted by the recruiting agent of the museum.

One midsummer night in 1938 while my Uncle Zon was on guard duty at the Heijo (Japanese name for Pyongyang under the Japanese occupation) Museum, some of the ancient treasures inside the museum were stolen by three or four intruders. My uncle first knew something was amiss when he suddenly saw a strong rope (about ¾-inch in diameter) swinging back and forth, suspended from the steel beams of the roof structure. Simultaneously he saw there was a hole in the roof roughly 1½ feet in diameter at the top end of the rope. He then realized that a group of robbers had entered the building through the hole, which had been temporarily created by contractors to replace a reinforced steel beam under the roof tiles. The robbers used a rope to slide down to the second floor of the museum and had proceeded to take out many of the treasures off the glass-enclosed shelves. As my uncle approached the swinging rope, he heard the sound of glass breaking. When the robbers saw my uncle running upstairs with a wooden, simulated Japanese samurai sword, two of the robbers wrestled with Uncle and threw a sack of hot pepper over Uncle's face and eyes so that Uncle was unable to carry on with the fight against them any further and fell to the floor with stinging eyes.

At that moment, there was suddenly a noise of many horses and the steel-wheeled carriages carrying equipment, led by a group of Japanese soldiers, outside the museum building on the cement road about fifty yards away from the entrance of museum. The robbers then started to climb back up to the roof using the suspended rope they had used initially. Perhaps they thought there was a group of police coming after them. As soon as they saw the soldiers with horses and carriages loaded with equipment, they panicked, and one of them fell to the ground from the rooftop, unable to move. Two (or three) other robbers managed to escape with an unknown quantity of treasure. By then my uncle became conscious enough to rush himself toward the front entrance of building and start pounding a large, brass disc (gong) with his wooden sword. The marching Japanese soldiers heard the noise of the vibrating brass disc, and they ran toward the museum entrance. Uncle was at first unable to clearly communicate just what had happened, and he became uncertain as to whether they were going to arrest him or help him. After they understood Uncle's explanation, however, they quickly washed his eyes with their canteen water and searched around the museum under the bright moonlight and found the robber lying on the ground who had fallen from the rooftop. One of the leading soldiers told Uncle that they were in the vicinity of the western slope of the mountain for a night combat exercise — they did not identify the exact location of their training exercise, and they were marching back to their compound approximately eight miles away. The solders then took the wounded robber to their compound and delivered him to the city's police headquarters the next day. Fortunately most of the lost treasures were recovered and returned to the museum within two months.

As of today, I am wondering whether the robbers were part of, or linked to, the construction workers or an employee of the museum. As they say, many crimes occur from those who are quite familiar with the inside settings of the targeted building.

The Heijo Museum was built by the Japanese authority of Pyong-an-Namdo (one of the thirteen provinces of Korea), which includes the Pyongyang metropolitan area and many other surrounding smaller cities and farming communities). The museum was built approximately two-thirds the way up the side of a nearly 800-foot-high mountain (called Moranbong) on the western outskirts of Pyongyang. A concrete, paved road approximately twenty-feet wide connected the base and the top of the mountain. It was open for all citizens of Korea, including organized, student-touring groups, civilian visitors, and local or rural citizens. Admission was free to all. At the top of Moranbong stood a 250-foot-tall castle (called Ul-mil-tae) with several firing holes on three side walls. The castle had been built during the Yi Dynasty Era to defend the city against northern intruders. It overlooked a panoramic view of the natural landscape, exhibiting the flow of the Tae Dong River, which is a major supply source of water for the city of Pyongyang.

The museum had a two-storied, high ceiling. It was an all-white marble and gray limestone structure, covering floor space equivalent to a medium-sized-city block. Although there was no air conditioning inside the building, it was amazingly cool during the hot summer. At the end of each hallway stood a portrait of the Japanese viceroy, Minami Jiro, in his army uniform. He served in Korea from 1936 to 1942 and was an advocate of the naisen ittai policy (the Japanese policy of cultural assimilation in colonial Korea).[4] All student visitors were required to bow to the portrait as they passed through. The front court-yard of the museum was landscaped in the Japanese style, being covered with white- and beige-colored, marble-sized gravel, with tall, white pines (an aver-age of twenty-five feet each) and colorful, maple shrubs (momiji) surrounding the courtyard.

In spite of the fact that the museum was established by the Japanese and it was prohibited by the public-school curriculum to include any Korean history, the museum displayed many ancient Korean treasures dating back to the thirteenth century, such as coins, armor, ceramic or brass art objects of the Goryeo Dynasty (935 to 1392) and Silla civilizations.[5] Ironically the museum had a section where it displayed a five-foot-long model of Kobuk-son (the famous Turtle Ship, also known as the first ironclad warship in the world) led by Admiral Yi Sun-shin (1545-1598), who defeated the naval force of Toyotomi Hideyoshi at the sea battles of Chin-tao and Ryo-chun though greatly outnumbered by enemy ships. Unfortunately Admiral Yi died in battle by a gunshot at age fifty-three.[6] Most of the upper-class stu-dents were inclined to salute the charcoal-sketched portrait of Admiral Yi. One day immediately after the organized tour, our third grade Korean teacher jokingly told us how Admiral Yi won the battle in the Sea of Japan. Of course there were many splendid stories about how Admiral Yi had won the victory at sea, but the teacher purposely omitted the true, historical de-tails from the lecture in the classroom, except for mentioning the legendary story about how he led his naval force to defeat the enemy from boarding his ship. The story is as follows:

> After the initial battle had transpired and a large number of enemy ships were sunk, Admiral Yi told the enlisted naval personnel to celebrate the victory by drinking much rice wine (Sho-ju) and to dance with their swords by pounding over the deck at night. The following morning the sailors found

that there were numerous hands and arms of enemy sailors that had been cut off and were lying on the deck from those who had swum across from their ships and tried to board the deck of the Turtle Ship and to perform a surprise attack against Korean sailors...." Throughout the entire story, our teacher never mentioned the word of "enemy" as "Japanese."

Elementary School Vacations

The school year began on the first of April, with students getting one week off between the school years. For the first two days of spring break, second-grade-and-up teachers and students were assigned to plant small trees on the mountains near the city. Using the planting technique and spacing of the trees between a given distance and area, kids were asked by attending teachers to calculate in their heads the number of trees and the spacing between trees they could plant. For those who got the right answer, they were awarded with a half dozen pencils engraved with green, tree figures. The technique they learned from the two days of work was also applied to their ongoing mathematics classes, such as learning how to equate fraction systems.

Summer vacation fell in July and usually lasted four weeks while the winter vacation fell in December and lasted six weeks. One to two weeks in the summer was devoted to some sort of Japanese government project for students in fourth grade and above. Usually the kids would carry shovels and picks to a Japanese military installation or factory like they were carrying rifles, singing marching songs as they went. The factories included the airport, air force installation, tank and truck production factories, and ordnance and ammunition production factories. I myself was assigned to work at the army truck manufacturing facility of Mitsubishi. For students fourth grade and above, the only time during the summer which we could really call our own and visit relatives or go to the seashore was the week or two that remained after the two weeks that were devoted to a Japanese government project. We were not allowed inside the buildings but were kept outside doing odd jobs, such as trash pickup, digging ditches, lawn keeping, and pouring concrete. We worked 6½ days per week, six hours per day. Although we did not really enjoy working 6½ days per week, we dared not express our dissatisfaction. Our only compensation was a free lunch, which consisted of white rice with a cherry center and a half tablespoon of salty anchovy on the side. After our day's work, we were expected to study for upcoming classes. During summer and spring, the elementary school kids would also learn to plant and tend gardens in a two-meter by two-meter per student portion of the school grounds. Mostly cabbages were planted (for kimchi) although radishes and carrots were usually also included. Sweet corn, tomatoes, cucumbers, squash, green onions, and potatoes were also grown. Fertilizer was human manure, applied after the last crops were harvested. At one point, I fell with a bucket of manure I was carrying on my shoulders to fertilize the ground.

Shortly after my first major illness (the one in which my grandfather, a specialist in traditional Oriental medicine, had put heated cups on my back), my father directed my grandmother to take me to his farm on the outskirts of Pyongyang. There were some nearby hot springs that people who were recovering from an illness or otherwise feeling poorly often used. As Grandmother and I left the train, which stopped approximately five miles from the family farm, I found it difficult to walk. For a while I stumbled along as best I could, but finally my grandmother put me on top of the collection of pots, pans, and other household goods on her back and gave me strict orders to hang onto her. Her arms, already encumbered by a suitcase in each hand, could not hang onto me, but fortunately I had the presence of mind to wrap my arms around her broad shoulders and hang on for dear life despite my protestations that both my mother and father would be very angry if they knew that I, a six-year-old boy, was riding his grandmother's back!

Nevertheless, my grandmother was a very sturdy, energetic woman who successfully carried me on her back until we were about a mile from our destination. Thereafter I was able to climb down and walk the rest of the way. The next few weeks were spent enjoying the hot springs until it was time to return home. By that time, I had nearly completely recovered my strength and was able to walk back to the train stop on my own with no assistance.

As previously indicated, Korean schoolchildren typically got six weeks of vacation during the winter, although only about one week of it would be free from any schoolwork and allow students to enjoy outside activities, such as ice skating, sledding, ice fishing, or playing different types of indoor games. The Ta-Dong River usually froze over with a thick sheet of ice, making it possible for one to sit safely on top of the ice with a little charcoal burner to provide a small amount of heat. The fish obtained from ice fishing saved many a poor soul from hunger, although as I was usually too flighty and active to sit still for very long, I was unable to make a contribution to the family dinner table by this means. Our other holidays from school were typically short (one day).

Regardless of the vacation period, students were still required to fill up workbooks and bring them to the school weekly to have the teacher grade. Usually the workbook contained mostly review questions from the subjects learned in the previous school year and a few important topics for the forthcoming school year. The remaining one week was spent in visiting relatives or going places with our friends or parents.

My Family Loses Its Mother and We Struggle to Survive

My father was a heavy drinker in his early years (before age forty-five). Drinking parties, especially the ones conducted on his friends' fishing boats, were likely to keep my father away from the house for one to two days, after which he would appear disheveled and red-eyed. Fortunately he recovered after my mother's death, probably realizing he had four vulnerable children to raise.

My mother, who had been in declining health since I was eight years old, became sicker each day, finally taking to her bed more and more frequently. Lumps began to form in her groin and under her armpits, and she moaned as she examined them. Her father, who was an old herbal healer, utilized traditional medicines to treat her, using cupping (acupuncture) but to no avail. Some months before her death, she lost her father when he was hit by a city van while he was out looking for my cousin Yong Soo. Yong Soo had been abandoned by both his father and mother and was living with my mother's father. His death at a local hospital after having been hit by the truck left her frantic and upset. My mother's illness did not improve, and it was suggested to my father by my mother's relatives that perhaps my mother's father was causing my mother to remain ill, inasmuch as he was buried in a rather inauspicious location. So my father arranged to have my grandfather's remains relocated to a spot that was about fifty feet away in a spot that had more sunshine in the winter and a better view of the surroundings. Shortly after his reburial, my grandmother found my mother scrubbing brick from a wall near the house that had partially collapsed. The water used to scrub the brick was cold, and she had no gloves to protect her hands. She insisted that she had to scrub the brick in order to repair the wall. Her mind markedly deteriorated after this episode, and her physical health declined even more. My mother's cousin, who was engaged to a resident M.D. at the local hospital, was only able to arrange for her fiancé to give her injections, probably for the intense pain she was experiencing throughout her entire body, as her condition was too severe to warrant any other type of treatment. She died when I was eleven years old.

My mother's funeral was a traditional one, which required that the family watch the body for three days until her grave could be carved out from the family's funeral mound in the mountains near the city. The funeral procession lasted the entire day and was attended by the family and my father's closest friends. Upon the return to the house, we discovered that my mother's half sister had stolen all my mother's clothes and other personal belongings so that there was nothing left to distribute to the rest of the family.

My father missed my mother, and often on Chusok or other days which were meant to commemorate the deceased, he would take food and liquor to her gravesite as an offering and drink there with his friends until I would have to plead with him to come back to the house.

My father, who was never terribly stable at the best of times, especially since my mother passed away, began drinking more and more to the point of alcoholism. His nightly carousing with his staff and friends from outside the compound became longer and more alcoholic, and he began to pay less and less attention to his children and family. I was often entrusted to bring back a bottle of sake or whiskey from a local tavern when supplies ran low in the evening. One evening when I was ordered to bring back a bottle of sake from the local tavern, I suddenly became aware of someone calling to me from a dark corner. Looking toward the shadows, I saw a man who had some facial deformities. I ran as fast as I could down the street and returned home by another route. Later we heard that there had been several other young boys whose penises had been cut off by a man who had tried to collect boys' penises in an attempt to cure himself of leprosy. It was with some sense of relief, therefore, that we greeted my stepmother into the family about a year after my mother's death.

I actually had two stepmothers. The first one, brought into the home about three months after my real mother's death, seemed like a very kind woman, although she was anxious to rearrange the household furnishings and give away or get rid of items that my real mother had had in the home. My father didn't like the changes to the household, so he asked her to leave. She was very heartbroken and told me, who was twelve years old at the time, that if they ever wanted her to return, she would do so.

My father then waited a year before he took a second wife, stepmother Hong, Kilsong. Stepmother Hong was a Christian young lady from the province of the Soesan (western mountain) village of Hongchun, a small village of 150 people. The village was within six hours walking of Pyongyang over hilly terrain. There was no major wedding festival, inasmuch as it was my father's second marriage and he had children from his first marriage. A simple record being placed at city hall gave my family a new stepmother.

The farming community in which my stepmother had lived had a certain amount of charm. The townspeople were very rural in outlook and experience. They gaped openly at the school uniforms worn by my brothers and me and would peer through the fence at the new arrivals who traveled from Pyongyang to Hongchun. The country people were impressed by the school uniforms and citified ways. Soon my family was introduced to the local streams where they could catch eels in the mud under the rocks. (I almost mistook a poisonous water snake for an eel however!) Having in-laws in the country had certain advantages. Some years when rice was short in Pyongyang, my mother's parents or brother would be able to smuggle a certain quantity of rice to our home. (After the communist regime took over, however, my stepmother's parents sometimes had to purchase rice or product from a neighboring village to make up the allotment that had been imposed on them by the government.) Hongchun was a village composed largely of Presbyterian Christians. My stepmother was also a Christian, which explained why she never actively participated in the Chusok ceremony and was kind to her stepchildren, unlike many other Korean stepmothers who were often unkind to their stepchildren.

Stepmother Hong was a good Christian woman, which she showed in her heart and her actions toward her stepchildren. As previously mentioned, remarriage after the death of a spouse was frowned upon, and the poverty of the country often led to intense competition between stepmothers and stepchildren for family resources. But our stepmother showered us with love and attention and kept the family together, even in the face of my father's increasingly heavy drinking. She ensured we were fed and clothed, that our house was clean, and that my father's parents were well-looked after. A neighboring village to that of my stepmother's parents' in Hongchun also rescued an American pilot and hid him in the barn, largely motivated by the Christian beliefs prevalent in that area of Korea. Unfortunately this fact was eventually discovered, and the home where the pilot was hidden was burned to the ground, along with a number of inhabitants, who were still alive when burned.

My mother's death occurred just prior to World War II, at a period of time when material items became increasingly in short supply. Although the Japanese administration had seen to it that Pyongyang had modernized water and transportation systems, the war activity in Asia meant that the supplies of rubber and gasoline were drastically reduced and that most available transportation was by rail. Local deliveries, such as those by the butcher or the fruit and staples peddlers, were via pushcart or horse cart. Consequently foodstuffs and basic commodities were often in short supply, and we sometimes went hungry despite my father's well-paid job, the efforts of the entire family in the vegetable garden, and the occasional chicken meal obtained from the coop despite the constant presence of stray dogs and foxes. Rationing was a way of life. My brother Youngchan and I were occasionally sent on visits to my stepmother's parents, who owned a farm in the country, to retrieve clandestine quantities of rice for our family consumption. "Clandestine" because transfers of rice from the farm to the city were strictly forbidden. At that time, Korea grew the best rice in the Orient, favored by both the Japanese and the Koreans, i.e., a short-grained rice that clumped together during cooking. Korea can only produce one rice harvest per year due to the short growing season, effectively limiting the supply that can be provided. This type of rice is quite different from the long-grained, nonsticky rice favored by the Chinese and Southeast Asian countries, which can be grown through three growing seasons. The Japanese administration, in its determination to obtain the best rice for its population, required that all Korean rice be transferred to the Japanese. In return the Koreans were provided with the less-favored long-grained rice taken from Taiwan. This exchange did not sit well with the Koreans, who were very fond of their short-grained, sticky rice (suitable for picking up with chopsticks), but they had little choice in the matter. Nevertheless, my brother Youngchan and I brought back enough rice via the rail system to keep our family fed for weeks at a time. Being caught could have presented serious problems, especially for our father, who could have lost his job.

However, there was one time when Youngchan and I were caught on our expedition to retrieve rice from the countryside. One time during our winter vacation, we were sent during to visit our father's cousin who worked on our farm in Yong-gang (about fifty miles west from Pyongyang) to bring back some newly harvested white rice. I was eleven years old, and my brother Youngchan was eight years old. On our way back from the visit, our cousin packed a few pounds' worth of rice in cloth bags and wrapped them around the waist of each of us thinking that our overcoats would hide the rice. Unfortunately at the checkpoint of the train station, both my brother and I were caught by the Japanese police and placed in the local police station. The following morning at his office, Father received a call from the school principal about our arrest. Father, as he was somewhat influential to city hall and a PTA member, was able with the help of his superiors and the school principal to bail us out over the telephone without any penalty, and we were sent home minus the rice.

I would also gather and bring back sesame seeds from my uncle's farm during the summer. Sesame seeds grow on a long, vertical stem inside a pod. I could gather the pods from a nearby field where they were growing wild. Once the pods were collected, they would be set aside to dry. After the initial drying, the pods would be opened, revealing the sesame seeds. The pods and seeds would then be winnowed by throwing the pod-seed mixture into the air several times, which would leave only the sesame seeds. The seeds would be toasted and crushed and stored in glass jars until they were needed as garnish for salads or stir-fry dishes or as part of other concoctions, such as yot or baked goods.

Meat was a rare treat also; little cattle raising transpired on the Korean peninsula due to the lack of space and available forage. Most of the cattle that were butchered were aged rice-paddy farm animals who were past their primes. Even so, this tough, grainy beef brought a premium price when sold door-to-door by the local butcher. The most accomplished housewives were those, so the story went, who could extract all the flavor from handling the meat, extracting the juices from the beef and using it to flavor their other dishes. My father occasionally went hunting (sometimes taking me with him) for pheasant and pigeon with a gun whose caliber was probably close to that of a BB gun or air rifle. Usually the children were not allowed to eat such delicacies as pigeon or pheasant, which were reserved for adults. (My father often told me I would produce twin babies in my later life if I were allowed to eat pigeon or pheasant!) There were occasional barn swallows that I was able to flush out of their nests inside the haystacks and roast over an open fire. And later after we had moved into the city-water compound, there was an occasional meal of chicken. But mostly we had very little meat or fowl, except what we could forage from the wild. My grandfather (paternal) who lived with the family was in charge of the vegetable garden. This was fortunate, inasmuch as the vegetable garden often produced the major source of sustenance during the periods of privation that followed the collapse of the Japanese government, as well as the institutionalization of the Communist Party. My grandfather would labor long hours during the summer months, wearing the jute-based burlap dress, which, though scratchy to the skin, was held away from the skin by a framework of bamboo structures. This arrangement allowed for the free flow of air through the burlap cloth and prevented skin irritation while allowing for freedom of movement.

I remember that when my father was raising chickens, sometimes many of them would die for no apparent reason. As the Koreans had never heard of putting antibiotics into chicken feed, the only medicine available was to use water in which hot pepper had been soaked. The chickens did not care for the taste of it, so sometimes it was necessary to pour the water down the chicken's throat directly.

Most of the protein available to Koreans at that time came from either fish or plant sources. Soybeans were used to make tofu, which was generally fried in slices or crumbled into soups with a bean- or fish-based broth. Corn was available also to be eaten with rice or beans, thus providing a complete source of plant protein. Fish could be bought at Inchon Harbor straight from the fishing boat and in many varieties. Several varieties of whitefish were available (mostly cod or haddock), as well as squid, octopus, and occasionally blowfish, or "fugu." Koreans have never had much taste for sushi, regarding it as "toy food" and unsuitable for the table, so the custom of fugu-eating, Japanese style, never really caught on. Fugu, of course, has long been eaten for the neurotoxic effects, which are said to be highly pleasurable. But the blowfish eaten in Korea was simply caught and cooked like any other fish, with no effort to exploit its enervating effects. Sometimes when poverty or a dearth of fishing boats reduced the availability of fish from the harbor, people would fish in the

Ta Dong River. Ice fishing during the winter was common, especially among the poor and older people. And of course, for those hardy souls who were willing to walk on the surface of Inchon Harbor during low tide, there were crabs and abalones to be retrieved. One had to be careful, though, not to get caught in the harbor when the tide was coming in. Several unwary souls were typically drowned every season trying to retrieve their supper.

Junkmen also plied their trade door-to-door. There was a strong demand for old rags, bones, and scrap metal to be sold to the clothing, paper, fertilizer, and metal industries. For this recycling effort to be cost effective, the premiums paid for the goods were necessarily low so the junkman could not pay very much for the items he retrieved. His chief drawing card to entice children to bring him these items was yot, or sesame seed candy, which was transported in large coils and could be cut easily with a scissors. Koreans at that time were unused to sweets of any kind, so yot was a rare treat. Children would wait anxiously to see the junkman with whatever odd scraps of metal, rags, or bones that they had managed to save and receive their allotted portion of yot, usually bought by the junkman from a bakery. The presence of this recycling capability was certainly useful to the community, which would otherwise have had a serious garbage collection problem on its hands.

Middle School during the Japanese Era (1937–1945)

Schools were used to instruct in government policies and show loyalty to and worship Emperor Hirohito as Living God. Korea was considered part of Japan, and students were expected to conduct themselves in absolute obedience to whatever they were told by their teachers. In addition, based on their war strategy in China, which emphasized conquering important cities of China and Manchuria, the Japanese government perhaps planned to use educated Koreans (mostly college graduates) as an occupational force in its invaded countries. During the Japanese occupancy in Manchuria, many educated young Koreans were sent to Manchuria under Japanese mission to establish close relations with the handpicked leader and his people. Koreans then identified themselves as Japanese — with newly issued government I.D. cards — and acted as the police force or as business leaders when dealing with the Manchurian people.

Middle school, as defined in Korea, was considered to be grades seventh through tenth, unlike the middle school of North America, which is typically defined as grades seventh and eighth. Most of the population of Korea during this time frame did not have an opportunity to go to middle school, as they were required to work to help support the family or to care for elderly relatives or younger siblings at home. My own mother never had the opportunity to go to middle school, which was the norm in those days. People who did not have the opportunity to go to middle school simply had to make their way doing farming, manual labor, factory work, or perhaps clerking in a retail business. It was not considered a mark of disgrace to not have gone to middle school, as there were no societal expectations which demanded it, and in any case, the competition to get into middle school was quite intense. Examinations were taken, much as they are taken now to get into the best colleges. Only about a quarter of the elementary school students made it into middle school, and the top middle schools were the objects of intense desire, much as admission to Harvard or Yale is in the U.S. today.

There were a number of different types of middle schools. Some middle schools were devoted to creating engineering professionals, without the full complement of academic courses which are expected today in most of the engineering departments of colleges throughout the country. Other middle schools dealt with the classics, such as Latin, Greek, and the humanities; still others were more in the nature of vocational schools, such as the agricultural middle school that my brother Youngchan attended briefly. I believe my father learned a sufficient amount of civil engineering through the experience he had at the watch shop repairing mechanisms, perhaps in combination with a technical middle school, to be able to adequately ensure that the Pyongyang water supply was delivered to the population as required and that it was adequately augmented and protected from a number of threats. I myself attended a middle school designed to produce teachers, although I only attended Japanese middle school for two years until the exigencies of the war drove the Japanese government to demand that all young men leave school and devote themselves to the war effort. All schooling above the fourth grade was summarily terminated, with the students being assigned to work for the war effort. I myself saw my schooling interrupted only to be sent to work at a Japanese air base performing maintenance on a variety of Japanese fighter planes. In some respects, I was lucky in that I was able to maintain a good job in support of the Japanese air force and help support the family with the relatively good earnings I was able to procure.

In additional to middle schools, the Japanese educational system included "professional schools" that were really middle schools, except that they were professional training schools (equivalent to the middle schools described above, except for training students to be teachers, engineers, accountants, agricultural specialists, or others). Professional schools started at the age of twelve or thirteen and were usually five-year programs. Most curriculums taught in the middle schools were also included in the professional schools. A graduate of the School of Education (a professional school) would be licensed to teach elementary school.

Because of the quota system of nationalities and scholarship-offering programs at professional schools, particularly at the School of Education in Pyongyang to which I applied, the entrance examinations were very tough. Typically unless the kid was from a socially prominent background and made top grades at elementary school, it would be difficult to get into any professional school. Teachers were very well-respected and made relatively high salaries —more respected than M.D.s. Competition was very fierce. Once the student was admitted to the School of Education, he would be given a scholarship through his entire school years until graduation depending on his scholastic achievement, The middle school, on the other hand, was a preparatory school for colleges, and there were not many applicants except for the kids with a prominent financial background. Consequently the entrance examination was relatively much easier than was the case for a professional school, such as the teacher's college.

In my experience of applying for the School of Education, the ratio of admittance versus the number of Korean applicants was roughly one out of fifty to sixty. Particularly in those days, however, there were not as many Japanese applicants as there were Korean applicants, and the quota system was set up in favor of Japanese students; they had a much easier chance of getting admitted.

To be admitted to the School of Education in Pyongyang, one had to pass written tests consisting of selective questions from all the subjects learned in fourth, fifth, and sixth grades and impromptu compositions in Japanese under given topics. Those who passed the written tests (six hours a day for two days) would be given tests for athletic abilities, such as doing thirty-plus push-ups, fifteen-plus high-bar chin-ups, broad/high jumps, and running one hundred meters within the national standard level for sixth graders. The next step was to pass a day of oral tests, usually containing questions surrounding various topics from three or four faculty members who sat around the applicant in the examination room. After passing all these tests, one had to pass the physician's physical examination. The final requirement was that Father had to submit certified copies of two previous years' tax returns to prove that his income level was above average, thus screening out poorer children. Because of such rigid requirements for entering higher education, many elementary school graduates with poor household income were forced to enter into the city's labor markets doing manual labor in industries or assisting farming communities at the age of twelve or thirteen.

My father expressed his admiration for the fact that I passed all the tests for both scholastic and athletic abilities when he read the names of the applicants of those who passed all the tests on the large, white sheet (written with a large "sumie" brush) and posted on the brick wall near the school entrance. It was the first time in my entire life I received verbal admiration from my father. Customarily fathers seldom expressed congratulations to their children, although the father was inwardly proud of his children. The reason for this was the concern that the children would be spoiled if they received too much of admiration from their parents or teachers and would cease trying harder for future betterment.

At last, there was one more test remaining for admittance to the school, which was the physicians' physical examinations. Unfortunately this resulted in my failure to be admitted to the school even though I obtained a score of ninety-eight on the intellectual tests and even though I managed to do more than thirty push-ups, did better on the high jump and broad jump, and ran the 100-meter track well within the national standard. After a series of physical examinations, the Japanese physician noted in his report that I had a hydrocele and a flat foot. As a result, I failed the entrance examination. A few months prior to the entrance examination, at the recommendation of my father's friend, who was a practitioner of ancient Chinese medicine, I had pulverized sage burned on top of an enlarged testicle three times in one week. Although it created great discomfort and pain at the time of burning, it did nothing to cure the hydrocele except for leaving a coin-sized burn scar on my skin. During my days of the entrance examination, I also wore my grandmother's white towel (embroidered with one hundred plus-marks of red needle work) over my stomach and inside my undershorts, away from other people's sight, as a good luck charm. (Such towels were worn by many Japanese soldiers in war zones during the war). Nonetheless, all these methods did not help in getting admitted to the School of Education in Pyongyang. My father cried when I related the results. Although I mentioned the possibility of going to a school of engineering or premed school, those schools would have cost too much money, and my father was very uneasy about my desire to pursue any higher education other than to pursue a career in teaching.

Being able to attend a desirable middle school (in those days, the teacher's middle school was the most desirable of all the middle schools) in large measure depended upon my father's willingness to help support the school through public taxes and with large donations. My father's relatively good position within the Japanese administrative structure was one factor which allowed me to compete for a spot in the teacher's middle school (called a college despite the fact that it was well-recognized that elsewhere college commenced with the completion of twelfth grade).

Fortunately under the recommendation of the principal of the elementary school and an evaluation made by the Provincial Board of Education, I was immediately accepted by the Pre-School of Education in Pyongyang as an associate. This was a middle school designed to produce teachers. The theory behind going there was that I would be accepted to the School of Education with the total credit hours earned upon transfer after two years of successful academic training. The school had a very good educational reputation throughout the city of Pyongyang, and the head of school was a Japanese who was most loyal to Emperor Hirohito and Emperor Meiji. I had to learn extensively about Japanese history, the 124 Japanese emperors' names, and the characteristics of their administrations. I attended this school between April 1942 and the end of 1943 (between the ages of twelve to fourteen). Despite my father's good salary, I needed to obtain a scholarship to finance my education costs. Although no scholarships were available for this middle school, it would be possible to transfer all my curriculum from this college to the final teacher's college, which had a similar curriculum.

Heijo Teacher's Middle School emphasized farming, military practice, physical training, history, and classic literature. The farming lessons began with the student being given a four-square-meter plot of land with instructions to raise whatever crops they wanted. Students were to weed and tend the crops, with the crops to be sold later in the city market and the money given to the student. Soil was fertilized with human manure obtained from the latrine. Occasionally I would slip while carrying the manure (I carried two four-gallon buckets on a pole) and dirty my clothes.

Military practice with bayonet and swords was emphasized in order to prepare for future military service, as well as to enhance physical toughness. We would sometimes go on forced marches for days, with no food or water, in order to imitate the Japanese army training. We would have to lick the dew from the grass. This would be done to imitate the sufferings of Japanese soldiers fighting in China, who often had trouble in receiving supplies and whose well water in China was often polluted. I had heard that the Japanese soldiers had had to drink horse's urine due to the lack of water. Despite the lack of supplies, the students would have to march even on the hottest days and ensuring that the gaiters, which they were required to wear at all times, were perfectly aligned with their pants seams. Otherwise they would be subject to physical punishment.

In the morning orientation meeting during the summer, students would be expected to bring straw rope (six centimeters in diameter and twenty centimeters long) and rub their bare skin (arms, backs, and chests — sometimes till it bled) on command in response to a timed command (one, two, three, etc.). This was done to toughen the body and spirit, the teachers indicating it would enable the students to avoid sickness.

Middle schools required all students to wear school uniforms with short pants and a jacket that identified the school and grade of the wearer. The coat had five gold buttons, which identified the school of the wearer, as well as section and grade. Upperclassmen wore long pants, lower classmen wore short pants. Summer wear included a white shirt collar. The uniform permitted ready identification of wearer, together with school, and kept misbehavior to a minimum.

Lower-grade students were required to salute upper-grade students. Otherwise the upperclassmen would kick or beat lower-class students. Often upperclassmen who made good grades would be assigned to lower-class students to help them with their studies if they were having difficulties, especially in mathematics or reading. There was no selected room for the upperclassmen to tutor the lower classmen, so they would typically go to the roof of the building to assist in the teaching sessions.

Upperclassmen were, in some measure, required to ensure the peace and security of the entire middle school. Sometimes the school administration would invest certain upperclassmen (usually the class leader and his band of followers) with the authority to correct lower classmen, with some physical punishment allowed. Students would practice giving orders, shouting so that the teachers could hear from one hundred meters away. If the teacher did not hear, the students would have to continually repeat the orders. My throat started to bleed from the intense shouting that would result from having to shout continually.

The lower classmen would be "initiated," or "hazed," until they learned to appreciate their relatively low ranking and the fact that they were expected to perform and act in ways that did not bring disgrace to the middle school or the classes contained within it. Competition for best grades was intense, with mathematics (trigonometry and geometry) being my main emphasis of study during my first two years of middle school.

There were inspection days in which the kids' haircuts, fingernails, and clothing were inspected, usually by upper classmen who had been delegated the job from the upper-class leader on behalf of the school administration. Dirty hair, dirty fingernails, or clothing in disrepair were reasons for sending students home until the matter was corrected. Sometimes hazing would be undertaken so that the lower classmen would learn that it was very necessary to do their homework and to not come late to class, both of which would disgrace the class. Punishment would typically involve a few licks with a bamboo swat or the holding of a chair above the head, usually out in the hallway. Sometimes the kids would be locked in the locker room for a couple of days. On the more positive side, however, the practice of "shaking down" kids for their money was unknown, and the upperclassmen provided a measure of protection against molesters or those who would take unfair advantage of the younger kids.

My main teacher in middle school was Japanese and had graduated from an advanced teacher's college. He had pale, white skin and was from Nigata. The snows in Nigata often reached to the rooftops, which meant that the students had to tunnel through the snow to be able to walk around. Nigata was next to the Sea of Japan and had a climate similar to Buffalo, New York. The teacher made his students memorize the Empress Meiji's waka (consisting of thirty syllables) and haiku poetry (consisting of seventeen syllables), as well as teaching Japanese history. He emphasized the fact that the Tokugawa regime, which moved the seat of the empire from Tokyo to Kyoto, was wrong. He made the students memorize all the old Japanese songs from that period, many of them by the empress. An example: "I woke up looking at this mirror, and my mind should be clear as a mirror," etc.

My teacher at one point was angry over the fact that a kid found an American newspaper in his desk and laid it on top of his desk. He made the kids perform punishing, physical tasks for some time. Later he was transferred back to Japan and went to live in Hiroshima. It was rumored that the teacher was actually an American spy who guided American bombers by means of a hidden, red light at night, guiding the bombers to the target. He later died during the Hiroshima bombing.

End of Japanese Middle School and Going to Work for the War Effort

After two years at the preparatory teacher's college, when I was nearly ready to graduate, I was sent to work at the nearby Japanese air force base. It was near the end of WWII, and most schools were shutting down (except for elementary schools), with the students being sent to work in the military or factories doing war-related efforts. Although Koreans had not been allowed to join the armed forces prior to World War II, they had been allowed to join the supply companies and building battalions and act as civilian police, proving far harsher than their Japanese masters, in some cases. Now, however, they were expected to participate fully in the war against the Americans. Some preparation for war had indeed already begun; each year the school would make a glider by the industrial-arts class. Thirty kids would pull on the glider until the glider and its pilot would be lifted sixteen feet off the ground for a period of time. Memorials to the Japanese soldiers, wherein the bones of the soldier would be placed in a white box on a table, and the students would bow and pray to the bones, also occurred at the school.

Having been dismissed early from Heijo Teacher's College, I went to work at Pyongyang Air Field, which was the local Japanese air force base. This was during the last half of my final year at the teacher's preparatory college and delayed my entrance into the School of Education Pyongyang teacher's college. All my classmates had similarly gone to work in military compounds or hired themselves into a war-related industry. When I was working at the Japanese AFB, I was charged with repairing the structural damage of planes that had been in battle and found their way back to Korea. However, when the planes with structural damage had been attended to, I was sometimes put to work disassembling, cleaning, and putting the airplane engines back together with any needed repairs. Usually the cleaning would entail washing the individual art in either gasoline or a caustic solution. There were no gloves to protect the workers' skin, and my hands were often severely irritated by the gasoline and caustic chemicals.

During the war, the U.S. bombed the Japanese AFB and burned up the various shop machines in the refurbishment area (lathes, milling machines, and other power tools.) My co-workers and I spent a lot of effort in the refurbishment area. The time we spent in refurbishing all the machines left them functional again, if slightly out of tolerance. The Japanese, knowing this, sent over a number of replacement machines, which were immediately put into storage. They remained in storage until such time as the Russians came and looted them, sending them back to the USSR.

I chose to join the air force base because it enabled me to live at home and bring my lunch to work. Work at the Japanese air force base was relatively well-paid for that time. I was given rations (rice), the equivalent of thirty dollars a month in pay, and cloth to make clothes. Most of this I brought home to my father to improve our family's well-being. Despite the rice rations and relatively good salary, however, toward the end of the war, our resources became even more strained, and my stepmother and I were forced to go to the mountains and forage for food. At times we even stripped the bark from trees to eat the layer of pith between the surface and the interior, which although it did not provide many calories, it provided vitamins and a sensation of fullness when cooked as part of a soup base.

I joined the mechanics training program at the air force base. I was in charge of a number of other students (youth training), including Japanese students recently arrived from Japan. Somewhat to my surprise, I discovered that there was a rift between the instructors at the air force base. There were regular Japanese officers who were instructors, as well as a number of Korean instructors who let it be known that Korea had been unfairly occupied by the Japanese. Japanese instructors (usually those who had received training a few years previously, not the Japanese officers) would punish Korean students, and Korean instructors would punish Japanese students.

The training at the air force base lasted six months and largely consisted of metal-fabrication techniques that would be used on the Japanese airplanes. We received instruction as to how to file and weld steel objects and rivet and bend aluminum sheet metal. Sometimes we learned how to weld buckets and cans for practice and how to rivet damaged Japanese airplane bodies. We also had to clean up the airplane engines periodically. Airplane skins would have to be washed — often by hand with no gloves and with hot, soapy water, which was very caustic. There was also a lot of physical exercise that was imposed on us as part of our training, and we were expected to execute our orders promptly and accurately. The Japanese officer instructors would usually teach from textbooks and command our undivided attention, in spite of the fact that our work schedules and physical training sometimes led us to feel very sleepy. Woe to the person (or class) who fell asleep — he might be beaten severely or forced to do push-ups or run a great distance before returning to class. Sometimes when doing push-ups in a particular posture (putting weight on the hands and arms), the instructors would kick the student's backbone. Although the Japanese "initiated" the Korean schoolchildren to make them tough, they did not "initiate" their own schoolchildren the same way. Typically the Koreans were tough enough to stand that type of punishment, but the Japanese students often could not stand it, as the Japanese kids had typically not been subject to this type of abuse previously. However, Japanese soldiers were often "initiated" brutally, with the end goal of making them tough.

In their efforts to toughen us up, the Japanese would force the students to beat one another, standing them in lines opposite one another. If the students did not beat one another severely enough, the teachers would take over, often beating the students who failed to beat others severely enough. Sometimes the injuries would be severe, such as broken jaws. Students would also have to run in the heat. Students who came in very late to the goal were told to run again and again, sometimes till they dropped. In normal exercise, if the students did not move their arms and legs correctly, the teacher would come over and kick the students. Despite all the hardships, it made the students stronger. The physical abuse to which we were subjected made us almost impervious to physical pain at times. For example, as part of our training, it would sometimes be necessary to use a cold chisel on thick steel. Using a sledge hammer with a handkerchief to protect the eyes meant that sometimes the hammer would slip and hit the hand. If the student could not cut the steel with the sledge hammer, it meant that he flunked the test and would have to repeat another six months of training. Allowing the hand to rest in cold water would reduce swelling and would permit us to complete our task. Specific body postures that were painful or difficult to hold (i.e., holding one's body at a specific angle) were emphasized when doing special work, such as riveting, and were made possible by the physical toughness that our intensive training induced. I remember the case of a Korean foreman who accidentally pierced his foot with a scribing needle. The man had very thin sneakers, and the needle pierced his foot, went through to his ankle, and protruded six to eight inches from his ankle. To remove the needle, he put his foot in a vise and pulled the needle out forcibly. The foreman stopped the bleeding by pounding the puncture point with a hammer.

After the training, the Japanese and Koreans mostly got along quite well (at least on the surface), except for occasional flare-ups. At one point, a Korean got "initiated" by the Japanese soldiers due to the fact that he had failed to come to work for three days. There was no telephone system available, so the foreman sent the MPs to search for him. They found him and suspended him horizontally for three days from the attic beams without food and water. After three days, he was taken down and permitted to resume his work.

North Koreans have hot tempers, but once they have vented their anger, they customarily return to being friends, with no recriminations or lingering resentment.

An example was the leader of the local "gang" of Korean workers at the Japanese AFB with whom I had conflict. The Korean workers, despite their years of living under the tutelage and domination of the Japanese, were still set apart — whether by choice or by lingering Japanese discrimination is difficult to say. All the Koreans, save myself, had formed a "gang" both for purposes of mutual assistance as well as personal defense. The leader of the "gang," a young man of about thirty named Song, was proud of his strength and physique. He had assumed his station as gang leader through a combination of aggressive charm and good humor, as well as the power of his fists and expertise in martial arts. He had browbeaten, threatened subtly (sometimes not so subtly), and occasionally dominated the other Koreans with sheer physical force into acknowledging him as their leader. All, that is, except for me, who resolutely refused to acknowledge his dominance. Despite repeated threats, I continued to go my own way as an independent spirit without paying homage or tribute to Song as my "leader."

One day Song challenged me to a fight. Having successfully fought his way to the top, Song figured he would make quick work of me, being taller and heavier, with a more imposing physique. He believed that he could pound me into eventual submission and proceeded to use his fists. The site selected was especially dangerous, as it was near railroad tracks and away from the prying eyes of the Japanese guards. Although the fight was brutal and left both parties bloodied, I managed to walk away without giving the satisfaction of dominance to the gang leader. From that day forward, the gang leader and I left one another alone, each going our separate ways until the end of WWII and the dissolution of the Japanese control of the air force base, as well as all of Korea. When the Japanese were finally replaced in the governmental hierarchy by Koreans, Song and I reacquainted ourselves and discussed what our future plans were. When Song heard that I was planning to attend teacher's college, he thought that was an excellent idea and resolved to also go to teacher's college. Although he finally was able to attend teacher's college and successfully graduate, he was unable to land a prestigious assignment within Pyongyang and was forced to accept a position in a small, rural school. Although Song and I exchanged letters for a few years, eventually we lost track of one another at about the time when I was headed for South Korea. But our intervening friendship, despite our brutal battle, was typical of many of the friendships formed by the young men of Pyongyang in the face of deprivation, war, and successive oppressive governments.

As I worked at an air force base, it was natural that I should become acquainted with the Japanese pilots and look up to them. Students would be required to wear headbands with "kamikaze" written on them every Monday to commemorate the miracle that saved Japan from Chinese ships centuries earlier. If students forgot a headband at home, they would be forced to run around the airfield till they dropped. At one point, I was given an opportunity to ride in a fighter plane from Heijo airport to Japan (the Tachegawa AFB). The pilot took care of his business in Tachegawa in a couple of hours and then flew back to Heijo (Pyongyang) airport. The ride made me airsick.

Despite my airsickness from that one fighter plane ride, however, I wanted very much to become a kamikaze pilot after I had been at the air force base for about a year. I was then age fifteen or sixteen. I went to the Japanese recruiting compound and took a written exam as well as the physical exam. However, they put me in a chair and spun me around, probably about one hundred revolutions. I failed the test due to the fact that I could not stand upright after the spinning in the chair. Had I succeeded, I would have been a first lieutenant in the kamikaze squadron and probably been killed during the war.

The Americans bombed in North Korea during the end of the war using B-17s. They had never bombed Korea during WWII except during the last week of the war when the Russians started invading in North Korea. They flew so high (about fourteen thousand feet or higher) that they appeared to be just a puff of smoke overhead. The bombs they dropped created serious damage to the airport, but the Japanese antiaircraft artillery did not come near the American planes, and we were left effectively defenseless.

However, the war ended with the bombing of Hiroshima (August 6) and Nagasaki (August 9, 1945) when I was sixteen years old. After the bombings, the emperor made a concession speech to the empire on August 15. Emperor Hirohito could not see that further civilian loss of life was worthwhile and conceded victory to the Allies. My Japanese foreman told me, "Until now the Japanese have been your older brother; now you will be our older brother, and we will be your younger brother. Perhaps in twenty years we will join our hands as equals."

Chapter V
The Russians Invade Korea

*A*pproximately two weeks prior to the end of WWII, from about the first of August 1945, the Russians had begun invading Manchuria and North Korea through the northeastern end of the peninsula. They began to cross the border of Siberia and Korea (bounded by the Yalu River) and engaged in battle against the Japanese troops in North Korea and Manchuria. About a week after the beginning of the Russian invasion, America dropped the atomic bombs in Hiroshima and Nagasaki, and World War II in Japan finally reached an end on August 15, 1945. Thereafter, Koreans observed this day as "Liberation Day." Immediately after WWII, Russia sent over thirty thousand troops as a post-war occupational force into North Korea. A year previously there had been an agreement by Churchill, Stalin, and Roosevelt at Yalta to divide Korea into two sections (North and South), although it was left to the generals in Washington to agree that the appropriate dividing line would be at the 38th parallel. The Americans post-war occupational force, on the other hand, did not land on South Korea until as early as six months after WWII.

The division of Korea did not please most Koreans. Most of those who had been dispossessed under the Japanese were happy that their conquerors had been defeated, and some of those, especially those who had been active in the revolutionary movement, were either Communists or persons who believed that perhaps Communism had advantages which should be examined. Others, especially those who had profited from the Japanese occupation, were horrified to think that the Soviet Union should be their new master. The Russians and the Japanese had been very much at odds since the Japanese won the 1915 war against the Russians in Manchuria and the Sea of Japan. War occurred when the czar was struggling with the Bolsheviks and could not reinforce the Asian troops. As a result, the Japanese expanded into Kamchatka Island (Karafuto) and the southern portion of Manchuria, thus dispossessing the Russians of some of their previous land holdings.

After the Russians invaded, they pretended that they were the liberators of the Koreans from the Japanese, although the Korean populace realized that it was the Americans who really liberated Koreans from the Japanese. At the beginning of the Russian invasion of Korea, they treated Koreans as they would the Japanese, i.e., as enemies. They ran down Koreans in the street with their vehicles and kept going. One example was the driving of a Jeep up to the top of a shrine in the Pyongyang City Park. Many Russian soldiers were ex-convicts from the Black Sea area and were given the opportunity to serve in the Russian Army. Those prisoners that were from Stalingrad often were the real oppressors of North Koreans. Those from Stalingrad had seen severe conflicts with the Germans and were often much more brutal than the ordinary Russian soldiers, and their superiors were, in many cases, apologetic about their behavior. Many Russian soldiers were illiterate, unable to read and write letters back and forth to home, and had to have their superiors read and write letters for them. However, they loved to sing, dance, and drink. They did not allow Koreans to sing their own songs, which they deemed as too dispirited and slow. Rather they taught their own Russian songs, which tended to be lively and dynamic, including songs dedicated to Stalin, Moscow, and the World Democratic Youth Song. Most holidays included singing this latter song. They treated the Koreans as equals and were able to communicate through Japanese and even learned some Korean. The Russians also tried to fraternize through the population (drinking with the populace) and would often try to communicate politely with the populace. (By contrast the Americans would often seek to learn the four-letter words connected with sex and would only try to communicate when seeking out a prostitute.) Russians drinking with the old men in the taverns was a very common sight; they sometimes even took the sweaters off their backs to pay for the drinks.

Nevertheless, as the Russians took control of the government, they began to transport the Japanese and their Korean sympathizers to the northern provinces of Korea and Siberia. Occasionally the Koreans would ambush the Russians after they had been out drinking and kill one or more at a time. Although the Koreans did not have any weapons, the element of surprise allowed them to kill the Russians with their bare hands.

The propaganda war by the Russians against the Japanese and the Americans, as well as other Western democracies, began immediately after the invasion. They totally took away religious freedoms and taught that religion eats up your life, especially the Christian religion, which was the "opiate of the people." The most commonly used example was of white landowners in the South who used it to pacify their black slaves and promise a reward in heaven. The Russians tried to persuade us that Christianity was the source of many wars and prevented the establishment of a just and fair government. They preferred to use the word "democracy" rather than "communism" or "socialism," even though the Russian concept of democracy was quite different than that of most Western societies.

The Russians attempted to indoctrinate the Koreans against the capitalist system, specifically the U.S. According to their beliefs, the Westerners had plundered the overseas nations and produced goods that the underdeveloped nations had to buy. "Down with the imperialists" was the cry. A dearth of overseas colonies to plunder caused the U.S. and others to create wars, so they reasoned. Russia wanted to extend its influence to China and Southeast Asia using the Communist ideology. The Russians labeled the U.S. and Japanese governments as evil out of fear of capitalism, which was able to perform the economic miracles that communism could not. The Koreans could not understand why the Russians hated the U.S. and Japanese so much. The answer was that the Russians could not successfully install their Communist government as long as the capitalistic governments of the U.S. and Japan existed. The Russians also wanted to extend their hand into the Southern Pacific islands, as well as Southeast Asia, to take free resources from those locations. Russians also introduced free education for all grades up through middle school. The only tuition required was for college, and Russians also provided many scholarships for college as well. School principals were often women (more than half).

The Russians did not bring their own food or supplies with them when they marched into Korea. Rather they stole most of the food they required, although they did bring some of their own medicine. They proceeded to try to indoctrinate the Koreans with Marxism, using loudspeakers that played both music and propaganda, as well as schools to do this. They began by teaching evolution, hatred of capitalism, and the Marxist view of history. They sometimes confused all three in their efforts to get their point across. They portrayed themselves as having sacrificed themselves for the benefit of the Koreans against the Japanese, thus providing rationale against their plundering of the Korean people. They used the schoolteacher as a propaganda tool to preach communism to the schoolchildren. The Russians emphasized the teaching of evolution, from the creation of one-celled ocean creatures to tadpoles, then to frogs, and then to land animals (birds and mammals). The evolution of the earth was traced through the Stone Age period, leading to the slavery society, which lasted thousands of years. That society was then transformed to a totalitarian society, which in turn led to the formation of capitalism, which robbed underdeveloped nations. War between capitalistic societies yielded to the imperialistic age, which bred socialism, ultimately resulting in the formation of communism. To further confuse their treatise on evolutionary science with political aspirations, they included a lecture about the transmission of malaria via mosquitoes. However, the Koreans were already well-aware of the association of mosquitoes and malaria via the Japanese and needed no tutoring on this score. Malaria used to be prevalent in Korea, and when I first acquired it, I managed to cure myself of it by running very fast till I finally fell down.

Under communism the dictate was, "From each according to his abilities, to each according to their needs." Russians did not consider themselves communists but rather socialists. Under communism, said the Russians, people would be given the opportunity to earn whatever they desired by the good offices of the government.

The Russians portrayed themselves as great saviors of Korean society, though the reality was the reverse. They tried to make the Koreans believe that the great Soviet army liberated Korea, although their very presence was a real burden to the Korean people. True to their Viking origins, the Russians had a way of stealing anything that wasn't nailed down. Theft of agricultural products was quite common, both for immediate troop consumption as well as for transportation back to Russia. They were likely to steal the produce and farm animals which even the city dwellers had managed to maintain under the Japanese. Many cows were killed and sent to Siberia for food, thus robbing the cows from the farmer, who often depended on the cows for pulling a plow. Much grain was stolen and sent back to Siberia as well.

At the Japanese AFB where I worked, the machine shop had burned up in an air raid during WWII. My coworkers and I tried to clean up the machine shop as best we could, cleaning the lathes and other equipment. We reassembled the machines to the best of our ability and generally made the machines functional. The Japanese firm in Osaka replaced the machines shortly thereafter, but the head of the machine shop wanted to use the old lathes for as long as possible and put the new lathes in storage. However, when the Russians came over and saw the new lathes sitting in the storage building, they stole all of them and sent them to Siberia. Any personal property which they could confiscate from the Koreans, whom they viewed as their enemies, would immediately be sent back home to Russia. They robbed gold from the North Korean gold mines as well as the North Korean dentists. They were fond of jewelry, anything gold, watches especially. Theft of jewelry and watches from civilians was also common, even on the streets. Some soldiers had many watches on each arm, which they eventually sent to their families in Russia. At one point, the Russians dropped all pretense of buying things and simply stole from the markets. I remember vividly seeing a woman Russian soldier and a Korean woman fighting viciously in the marketplace over a quantity of goods. They began pulling each other's hair, and the two women fought it out despite the presence of the Russian men soldiers, who possibly could have intervened to help their comrade.

Koreans wondered why, if the Russians were such a great country, they were having to steal watches and other goods from the Koreans. The answer, of course, was that the Russians were much poorer than the Koreans had been under the Japanese. People who spoke out against this system wound up being sent to Siberia. They attempted to portray themselves as setting up a society wherein the ordinary worker would live much better than he or she had under the Japanese. Of course most Koreans did not believe this and pointed out that they had lived better under the Japanese and that they had less to eat and fewer material possessions under the Russians. Such people were captured and sent to prison camp or Siberia.

The Russians brought in a fake Kim Il-Sung, an imposter of the original guerrilla leader. He did not speak Korean very well at first, coming into Korea as a Russian lieutenant. Although the Koreans recognized that the impostor was much too young (approximately thirty-two years old) to be the real Kim Il-Sung (who would have been forty-five to fifty years old), those who spoke out loudly were sent to the Siberian prison camps, where they lasted three to four years on average. Another city water employee and I were both at the stadium near Moran-bong Park when the Russians introduced Kim Il-Sung to the thousands of Koreans who had found their way into the stadium. The Russians introduced him as the legendary freedom fighter and recommended that he be elected as the Great Leader.[7] Of course the populace as a whole recognized this as a Russian trick, but they had little choice but to go along and elect the Russian imposter as Kim Il-Sung, the Great Leader. I was required to teach my students a song that extolled the beauty of Korea and the virtues of the Great Leader, entitled "Kim Il-Sung."

Russians would walk into Korean houses in the middle of the night, claiming to be doing an investigation. The families would wonder what they did wrong. The police would not claim that they had done anything wrong but would claim that there needed to be an investigation. They would take the husband away, with no word as to when he would be released, and the family would never hear of him again. No word would come as to whether the man was shot or sent to Siberia, but it appears as if most of them were sent to Siberia for forced labor under harsh weather conditions, as well as harsh environmental conditions, as many of them wound up working in sulfuric acid plants or similar enterprises. Most died within three to four years in the concentration camps. Sometimes the people who would be sent away were the parents of my students, but there was nothing I could do to alleviate the situation. Due to the extreme hardships of Korean life, suicide was not uncommon. Jumping off a cliff was most usual, as was lying down on the railroad tracks and allowing the train to run over one's body.

Japanese women were subject to rape under the Russians and soon took to dressing like men and cutting their hair very short, sometimes into crew cuts. This did not necessarily help, as some bad Koreans would point their fingers at the Japanese women, regardless of whether there were husbands nearby. They would inform on the Japanese as to where they were hiding and pointed out where the riches of the Japanese were hidden. Before long the Japanese were rounded up and sent to Siberia or concentration camps within North Korea. Russians would also rape Korean girls, as well as married women. They would put a blanket over the husband's face and gain entrance to the home by virtue of their automatic weapons. Many of the girls were virgins, premarital sex being then very uncommon. The rape of Korean women was in sharp contrast to that of the Japanese soldiers in Korea, who typically visited houses of prostitution rather than trying to have affairs with Korean women or raping them. Sometimes five to six Russian soldiers would rape a single, virgin girl at once. Eventually the populace would pound pots and pans to create a noisy atmosphere, as well as alert people to their presence, and drive the Russians away. Russian women would also take Korean men aside for trysts and sometimes did not even wear underwear. The Russian women were not able to have affairs with their own soldiers, so they took their opportunities to have sex with the Korean men. As a rule, the commanding officers would punish the soldiers severely if they discovered that their troops were committing such acts.

Of course there was no point appealing to the government for help in stopping the raping and pillaging that followed in the wake of the Russian invasion. The Russians would simply be cleared by the "People's Democratic Court" with a jury selected by the government. The trial was announced through a loudspeaker, and the entire trial would be broadcast over the loudspeaker. The outcome of all trials was predetermined. Most offenders (guilty or not) would be sent to jail or Siberia. A few cases involved execution, and executions typically were not broadcast, although execution pictures would sometimes be published in the press. Theft or other property crimes were normally winked at as being "ideological crimes," whereas true ideological crimes (e.g., political "crimes") were normally punished severely.

Despite the rapes of the Japanese and Korean women, another thing that the Russians introduced was the concept of women's liberation. They tried to ensure that women should stand on their own two feet. They introduced women into positions of power that they had been previously denied. They tried to persuade women that they had been oppressed and should play a fuller role in society. The Russians took steps to ensure that women should become school principals, doctors, etc. Chaoi Sung Hee, a famous Korean ballet dancer, was brought from Moscow to take over a government post. Although she was originally educated in the U.S., she later went to Moscow for additional training. The Russians gave her a good position in the government and later made her a minister in the North Korean government. When husbands and wives argued and the men started throwing dishes, women would also begin breaking dishes. When the husbands would ask why the women were breaking dishes, the women would reply, "If you break one dish, we also break one dish." Even though people might consider this a laughing matter, it really happened that way. If men mistreated women, reports of this to the Russians or North Korean government would cause the men to be deemed "politically unfit" and sent to a labor camp.

In their desire to spread socialism and a "fairer" distribution of wealth, the Russians took land away from the Korean landlords in a land-reform activity. Landlords who owned houses for rent were likely to be jailed. My father had farmland near the seacoast in Yongdon, which my father's cousin managed all through the Japanese occupation. My father had originally started out with a small farm (six acres) and then, through his savings and additional buying and selling of houses, managed to buy more farmland till he had acquired approximately forty acres, a rather sizeable holding for that time. At the end of the year, anything left over would be divided between my father and his cousin. The Russians took the land away from my family and gave it to his cousin and chopped down the apple trees, refusing the rights of the landowners to control what crops they produced. They asserted the rights of the government to dictate the crops to be produced — in this case, rice and beans in place of apples, which they declared an unnecessary luxury. Other landowners were lucky in that the people working the land would share the profits with the landowner. However, my father's cousin did not attempt to pay rent for the land in spite of the fact that many other tenant farmers did pay rent to the original landowner. An old Korean saying was that "friends are sometimes much better than family." My father was heartbroken, but there was nothing he could do to reverse the situation.

However, despite their larcenous ways, the Russians believed that everything needed for life should be produced locally, whether it was farm produce or factory goods. They did not want the populace to become fond of Western products, which they viewed as a corrupting influence. Restaurants, cinemas, and department stores were viewed as bourgeois, worthless influences, and to be avoided. Due to the galloping inflation, the populace had far less money to spend on such luxuries and so obeyed, in large measure.

Although my family lost much of their savings due to currency conversion, my father obtained a promotion to the position of city water commissioner and was able to move to the Japanese manager's house in the city water area, which contained storage tanks and pumping stations. However, this was not entirely an unmixed blessing. The Russians stole two pumps out of the stations, which caused water shortages throughout the area. They occasionally sent MPs to threaten my father with death if he did not keep the Russian troops amply supplied with water. However, the house inside the compound was very comfortable in comparison with our previous environs. Our status inside the compound was safe from the predations of the Korean police and the rogue Russian soldiers who were loose on the streets of Pyongyang.

Life in the City Water-Tank Compound
The city water area was located near the west end of the city and was administered by city hall, which at that time was somewhat independent from the rest of the political infrastructure that the Russians were trying to establish. After my father's promotion to city water manager, all five of the city water employees except one, plus my family and uncle, all lived within the compound. The compound was approximately a thirty-acre lot. It was very nicely landscaped, with three buildings in total, including our house, as well as one which was a housing facility for the employees. The remaining building was eventually used as a makeshift facility for the Russian guards, who rotated through the compound. The Russian compound was about eighty yards away from my family's house.

Our house was full with four kids, my stepmother and father, as well as my father's side grandparents and occasionally my uncle. One bedroom was occupied by Youngchan and I, another room occupied by my father and stepmother, another room occupied by Inchon and Heechan, and another room occupied by my grandparents. Although a bit crowded, our house was a far nicer one than any in which we had lived up until then.

Although my father had an important position which paid relatively well, the threat of hunger was never far from our minds — or from the rest of the Korean people. Crop failure in Korea meant that the population would eventually be forced into the forest to eat grass and the green bark of the trees, a practice which continues in North Korea until this day. With an eye to frugality and the best use of resources, my father lost no time in installing a huge garden and chicken coop in his front yard, which was an important source of food, especially in the lean times just after World War II. My grandfather and all of us kids worked as best we could to assist in helping to put food on the family table, using the contents of our indoor, nonflushable toilet to spread over the garden for fertilizer. I, as the oldest child, was expected to not only ensure that order reigned among my other siblings but to elicit their help in taking care of the garden. I was also expected to ensure that no foxes or dogs encroached upon the chicken coop, which held up to a hundred chickens at a time. Occasionally a stray dog or fox would injure a chicken, and I would have to dispatch it by chopping off its head and consigning it to the stew pot. For awhile we were able to help put food on the table, and it relieved us all immensely to be able to assist my parents in this manner.

The city water area had a stone wall around it and an iron gate at the front, with entry strictly controlled. The area contained three or four large cement city-water tanks with underground walkways between the tanks. They were designed and built in the 1920s by the Japanese administration. Unfortunately due to lack of maintenance, the cement seams had begun to crack and started to produce small streams of water, which leaked into the street below. Some Korean women came to wash their clothes in the leakage area, taking advantage of the free water for which they would otherwise have been expected to pay.

The Russians guarded the area to prevent enemies from poisoning the water supply. They were concerned with anticommunists in the area or the South Koreans making an intrusion into the area, either poisoning it or blocking it off. My father was once in a position to try to save his neighbors during massive flooding near the city-water compound area. (This occurred in the time shortly after the Russians had invaded.) My father had the Russians tie a rope around his waist and then lower him approximately five feet down from the bridge that crossed between the water compound area to the bank opposite where the main city of Pyongyang was. He managed to pull off children who were floating down the river, clinging to the roofs of their houses or other debris. Similarly he was able to capture some farm animals and get them safely secured on the bridge. Although the Russians were usually circumspect about allowing access to the city water area, they did not interfere with the worshipers who visited the Buddhist Japanese shrine, which was located in the city park area, Moran-bong, down below. I recall seeing a group of gamblers "take over" the little fortress Ul-Mil-Tae in the park. (This was the structure the Russians drove their Jeep up to.) The structure was a fortification that was used to shield archers against Chinese attacks, having slits in the wall, and was only approximately five feet high. The gamblers preyed largely on the rustic farmers both before and during the Russian occupation. They usually traveled in packs of six men looking for an easy mark. Usually the farmers would be suckered into a type of gambling that involved the unwrapping of a series of numbers from a pencil. The farmers might win a little in the beginning, but as soon as the stakes rose, they would be swindled out of every last bit of money. The Russians did not normally participate in gambling, inasmuch as they had little need to obtain Korean money by illicit means; they controlled the monetary printing presses and always had plenty of cash. However, they were nevertheless subject to theft. Leaving aside the drinking orgies that would make them susceptible to being hit over the head and forcibly robbed, Russian troops, both enlisted men and officers, would often take Korean public transportation, unlike the Americans who drove everywhere in their Jeeps. Traveling on crowded Korean trains and buses made the Russians ideal targets for pickpockets, and many Russians quickly found themselves relieved of their cash. This was not a major hardship, however. In those days of rampant inflation, all that was required was to print additional currency.

The park was very beautiful, and life in the compound was enjoyable although there were some hazards associated with our location. While we were living in the city water compound, the Russians often visited my father with their automatic weapons. On one visit, they killed a large, black, shiny snake that was climbing up the steps to the house with their automatic weapons. My father was horrified and told the Russians that they had killed a "good luck" snake, one that was not poisonous at all and that brought blessings on the house.

Another time the Russians used their automatic weapons to shoot at a flock of geese flying overhead. Despite my father's objection that the geese were protected by the government, the Russians presented him with two geese and told him to feed the family.

All stray dogs that entered the compound were immediately shot. They were invariably given to one of the water-compound employees who had tuberculosis. Dog meat was reputed to be particularly strengthening for tuberculosis patients.

The presence of the heavy drinking Russians was also a source of concern to our family. Although his marriage to our stepmother had made our father somewhat more stable and less prone to drink heavily, there was always the danger that he could slip back into his habit of heavy drinking when experiencing pressures at home or at work, though I am glad to say that to the best of my knowledge that did not happen.

For the most part, the Russian guards were decent people — most of them were at the compound for two to three months each, with twenty of them living at a time in the compound in the spare building that was unoccupied by either the family or the Korean city water employees. The spare building where all twenty soldiers slept was covered with Japanese straw mattresses but was otherwise unfurnished except for the cooking facilities. The cooking facilities amounted to no more than a wood fire upon which to cook their soup and boil hot water. The soldiers ate only two meals per day: an 11 A.M. breakfast and dinner from 9 to 10 P.M. They came to our house for their weekly baths, as our house was the only one with washing facilities, as crude as they might seem by modern standards. (Our bathtub was cast iron and heated from below by means of a wood fire.) They were very polite when asking to use the facilities, and the family was happy to oblige, as they were respectful, and each soldier spent only fifteen to twenty minutes in the tub.

Captain Kruschev was in charge of the troops who inhabited the city water area. He was in his late forties, had a deep voice, was six-foot-five, and very good-looking. He was there for the entire Russian occupation and did not rotate, unlike his subordinates, who typically rotated after about two to three months in the compound. He drank with Father and socialized with the family. He asked Father for introductions to Korean women. My first introduction to sex was seeing Captain Kruschev on top of a Korean woman that Father had brought to the house, sleeping in my grandparents' room. When I mentioned this to my father, I was told to keep quiet about it!

The Russians for the most part were quite friendly with the Korean people and made an effort to be hospitable and helpful. They had brought medicine for malaria and worms, which was helpful whenever anyone in the family was ill with either one of these diseases. Usually there would be a party when a contingent of them departed, and Father would be invited to drink with them. The soldiers would play old Russian songs and do old Russian dances. We were often invited to eat with them — usually potato soup together with dark, Russian bread. The bread had a hard crust, which enabled it to be used as a pillow for their heads, and was sweet, being made with honey. Occasionally one of the Russians would pull out a slab of salt pork from his shirt to accompany the soup and bread. I rarely took a piece of salt pork, as it appeared to be uncooked, but the potato soup would usually produce diarrhea the next day, probably due to the excessive grease it contained.

I found the Russians to be generally good-hearted, although sometimes coarse, and often uneducated. Most of the Russians were illiterate, having to have their superiors read and write their letters, although there were a few who were able to teach our family how to speak, read, and write Russian. We found their clothing peculiar in that they wore gaiters that wrapped around their feet rather than socks. The gaiters that wrapped around their feet, of course, did not fit on top of the boots, as is true of most Western-style gaiters. We had an apricot tree in the back yard, ten to twelve inches in diameter, that used to produce lots of apricots. However, the Russians came over and shook the trees, trying to get more apricots, and sometimes climbed up the tree and broke the branches to get at the fruit.

The Russians each had a horse. One afternoon I helped the sergeant in charge wash the horses in the river on the foothill side of the city park. In the process of washing one horse, it stepped on my foot, not letting go till I screamed for help and the sergeant came to my rescue. After we were finished washing the horses, the sergeant invited me to visit the Russian soldier's compound approximately three miles away, which was located below the city water area. He invited me to ride one of the other horses, but that horse, evidently sensing my status as a novice rider, nearly succeeded in scraping me off his back by purposely walking under the pine tree and causing my neck to be caught in the pine branches. The soldier thought this was very funny and taught me how to avoid being scraped off by the branches in the future. We rode three miles to the soldier's compound, where I was offered some dark bread as well as a bucket of water that the horse had drunk from that contained straw on its surface. I politely declined to drink from the bucket, but the Russian soldier did so anyway. At that point, I really thought the Russians must be barbarians!

Despite their damage to the apricot tree, however, the Russians helped my family quite a bit. Because monetary inflation due to the excessive printing by the Russians was a serious problem, it was necessary to carry pockets full of money to the market to buy groceries. My father's wages were not quite sufficient to pay for our expenses, and since his land had been stolen from him, Grandmother's earnings from the concession stand where she sold apples near the city water compound next to the city park really helped. Her earnings often helped feed the family and meet daily expenses. Unfortunately Grandmother's earnings were destroyed during the inflation and currency exchanges. We went from three meals a day to two meals a day to one meal a day. A second monetary exchange destroyed our small savings totally. Our living status was much reduced in comparison to what it had been under the Japanese. During the second monetary exchange, the government set a limit of 150 won that could be exchanged initially, and thereafter a specific amount could be exchanged each month. This lasted about ten months, and thereafter the exchange system was closed down totally. This meant that Grandmother's savings had been almost totally wiped out. Grandmother had to walk down to the market area to buy goods for sale near the city park. Nevertheless, since other Koreans would have considered carrying apples for Grandmother's concession stand to be plebeian and unrefined (contact with merchandise degraded them), I tried to avoid this task whenever possible. However, the Russian soldiers would sometimes help carrying apples for Grandmother. They would also cut trees for firewood and split them into logs. The Russians also helped by shooting the occasional wayward dog that invaded our compound and killed our chickens. They would thereupon deliver the dead dog for meat to be consumed by the worker who was suffering from TB.

Nevertheless, especially toward the end of their stay in the compound, one or another of the Russian soldiers would occasionally endanger me or others in our family, either through their own carelessness or through their uncertain temperament. One example was the time we all were invited to dinner (the usual potato soup with bread). An emergency required the Russians to report to their own compound. They lined up and put their rifles on their shoulders. One of the soldiers tried to put his rifle on his shoulder, and suddenly the rifle went off, firing a number of shots suddenly. He wound up shooting himself in the foot due to the lack of a safety lock on his gun and had to be carried down to the compound.

On another occasion, one soldier began crying over the fact that it was his birthday. He had no one to celebrate with —his family had all died in Stalingrad. I tried to encourage him to adopt a positive frame of mind, but it was depressing, nevertheless, and more than a little frightening in that I was afraid that he might turn his gun on himself or even possibly me!

One other time, a Russian soldier who had been previously friendly with me pretended he was going to shoot me for singing while running laps around the compound. I raised my arms, playing along with him and thinking it was a joke, but the Russian really did fire. Thankfully he fired a blank, and it left me unharmed. The Russian thought it was a tremendous joke, but I was unnerved, nevertheless.

A second group of Russians came to replace the first group, who had transitioned without incident. Russians loved to drink and sometimes came to the compound to drink with Father, either Korean sake or vodka. They invited my stepmother to drink. She accepted the drinks with reluctance, never having consumed much alcohol. My father had been drinking since early evening and was asleep on the floor. The sergeant tried to rape my stepmother in the bathroom, but I prevented it by grabbing the sergeant's collar and pushing him away and telling all the soldiers to leave the house. Unfortunately Capt. Kruschev wasn't there. When he came back from Russia, the captain promised not only to punish the sergeant but gave my father a pistol and taught both my father and me how to use it outside the city water compound. From the previous examples, it can be seen that the Russians were human beings like anyone else.

Russians had stayed in Korea for two years until the North Koreans established a government to their liking. The Russian guards who had become almost a part of the family were beginning to withdraw back to Russia. Just prior to their departure, I found a Russian sergeant and his soldier-mistress in my father's office sleeping on a straw mattress together, the woman in a white gown. Soon after the North Korean police moved in during the establishment of the Democratic People's Republic of Korea (during 1946-1947) and stayed until I left for South Korea. Security was very much tighter than under the Russians, with the Koreans checking the family very carefully. No visitors from the outside were allowed into the compound. They did not help my grandmother in carrying her apples to the concession stand; indeed a contingent of them came and closed down her stand, saying it was an inappropriate activity. The family was happy to be still living in the compound, however. Just before I left, the DPRK police began building a radio tower about one hundred yards from our house.

Endnotes

1. https://en.wikipedia.org/wiki/Amaterasu
2. https://en.wikipedia.org/wiki/Imperial_Regalia_of_Japan
3. https://en.wikipedia.org/wiki/Yamata_no_Orochi
4. http://www.koreatimes.co.kr/www/news/opinon/2015/12/165_82414.html
5. https://en.wikipedia.org/wiki/Goryeo 6. Hiroshi Aoki, *Recent History of Japan, China and Korea* (Japan: Gentosha, 2003), 19. (日本、中口、朝鮮 ；近現代史；青木裕司)
7. David Halberstam, *The Coldest Winter* (New York: Hyperion, 2007), 74.

Chapter VI
Korea Is Partitioned and the DPRK Is Born

*R*ight after Hirohito's surrender (done out of a concern for Japanese life), Korea became independent. For the first three years after the surrender of Japan, the Russians and Americans faced off across the 38th parallel. Although the original agreement between the U.S. and Soviet Union was that there would be an election that included both Koreas within five years, the U.N. had given *the U.S. three years (until March 31, 1948) to achieve an anticommunist government.* On May 10, 1948, and on July 17, 1948, South Korea conducted national elections, which were opposed by the Soviet Union. The government resulting from these elections brought Syngman Rhee to power as president. Upon coming to power, Syngman Rhee immediately expelled terrorists and Communists from the nation of South Korea. These elections were countered by the North Korean elections of August 25, 1948, which brought Kim Il-Sung (the imposter) to power as the premier of North Korea. The Russians withdrew from North Korea in 1948 while the Americans withdrew in 1949. However, in April, 1950, Kim Il-Sung visited Moscow and obtained Russian permission to try to reunite Korea. Toward that end, the North invaded the South on June 25, 1950. The Americans hastily returned to Korea and at one point attacked Pyongyang, trying to bring the regime to its knees, but the North Koreans were reinforced by both the Russians and the Chinese, who refused to permit the U.S. and U.N. to remain in North Korea.[1]

After the establishment of a North Korean government in 1947, the Soviets began to withdraw their troops from North Korea except for their military/political advisors and technicians. Likewise the American troops and civilian workers also withdrew from South Korea. After the Russians invaded, Kim Il-Sung was posted by the Russian Army as the leader (premier) of North Korea in 1947. As the country was established as the People's Democratic Republic of Korea, Kim Il-Sung became president. Of course the person presented as Kim Il-Sung was not the same Kim Il-Sung who had fought for Korea's freedom in Manchuria against the Japanese. The Kim Il-Sung who was presented to the North Korean populace was much younger than his namesake and may have been from the Soviet Union originally.[2] Very few dared point out that this Kim Il-Sung was an impostor, in fear of being transported to Siberia. The new government created under this new Kim Il-Sung paralleled the Russian government in many important respects. He created seven ministries, including the ministry of interior, ministry of defense, etc. One minister was Choi Sung Hee, who was a dancer. She had performed in the U.S. and received many worldwide awards although exiled from Korea. She went to Russia and studied at a dance school and created a dance style that was half Korean, half Western (classical ballet).

The stated objectives of the North Korean government, formed in concert with their Russian allies, were perhaps not so different from many other governments formed in response to colonization from without. The DPRK sought to form a purely Korean government, eliminating all foreign influences, especially Japanese influence. The DPRK was intended to be a government that stood on its own without being subject to the predations of the Japanese — or for that matter any foreign Western powers, especially the U.S. They sought to instill a "fair" government, one which would remove the obstacle of extreme poverty, spread the wealth, and yet permit the government to be self-sufficient and not beholden to any outsiders. The government also sought to remove any disruptive influences that would prevent it from achieving its stated objectives.

In order to achieve its aims, the North Korean government began by taking over the schools and reorienting the traditional social structure. The traditional middle school structure was revamped and enlarged such that all persons in the country were not only guaranteed the possibility of finishing high school but indeed were expected to do so. The North Korean government well recognized the fact that in education lay the seeds of future prosperity. All members of society were expected to foster this aspiration and make it their own. Not only that, but the subjects taught, as well as the teachers themselves, were intended to further the advancement of the nation with government being the arbiter of not only the subject matter but the method of presentation of all types of courses taught. Free education was instituted for all grades up through high school, with scholarships available for college. (Women got more scholarships than men because they were trying to promote women's progress.) The government stressed women's rights. Women were allowed to be teachers, managers, and doctors, in contrast with the previous conservative Confucian philosophy that had kept women largely homebound. Schoolchildren were indoctrinated thoroughly with communist philosophy, as they knew no difference, not having experienced the Japanese government. Loudspeakers blared Marxist philosophy interminably at every opportunity. However, preferring to focus on the mental aspects of personal control, physical punishment in the military and schools was discouraged, unlike the Japanese regime, which freely used physical discipline on its soldiers. Schools also did not usually punish the students physically. The North Korean influences on education were very much influenced by the Russian Communist party at first; later on the North Korean government took the Russian precepts to an even higher level with respect to implementation of pure Marxism.

To celebrate its new sovereignty, the government created a huge monument in the Moran-bon city park near my home. Our home in the city water compound was about a ten-minute walk from the park, which was a very scenic place. It contained a hill, as well as a river passing at the base of the hill. The river continued outside of the park almost all the way around Pyongyang. The monument, which was at the top of the hill, was crowned with a statue of Kim Il-Sung. The monument had four sides, each side with a different portrayal of an incident in Korean history. The first side had a portrayal of the Russian sacrifices for Korean freedom; the second side had a portrayal of the worker's efforts to create freedom within Korea; the third and fourth walls also had designs carved within them, commemorating different features of Korean history.

I had begun teacher's college during the Russian occupation and had almost completed it by the time the DPRK had taken over. I was cautiously optimistic about the change in government, believing that perhaps I was being given a wider field of opportunity, and I applied at once for the teacher's college, which was five miles from home and located on the other side of the Ta Dong River. It was about a thirty-minute commute, and I would change trolley cars twice. I felt as if I were well-prepared scholastically due to my time at the preparatory teacher's college, and my flat feet and hernia would probably not keep me from enrolling under the new government auspices. I knew several of the teachers at the college, having had them as instructors at middle school. Those two facts enabled me to enroll in this upper-level teacher's college, the Pyongyang Teacher's College. The school had a capacity of 1,500 students and was located in a brick building. Curiously I met two former coworkers from the Japanese AFB, including a former antagonist from the Japanese AFB with whom I had previously fought but with whom I later became good friends. My brother Youngchan at that time was enrolled in the school of agriculture, which was much farther from the center of Pyongyang and required him to walk much farther from home.

The teacher's college was experimental in the sense that it had both male and female students (although in separate classes). During the time after the war, the North Koreans increased the amount of mixing between males and females in schools and at work, as well as society in general. I managed to finish the school curriculum in three years instead of the normally prescribed five years, having had previous classes of equal or greater difficulty in the same area at the preparatory teacher's college. The school emphasized the "inductive" method of teaching, which emphasized the operation of logic and reason rather than rote memorization. The inductive method was intended to help the student arrive at the correct solution rather than simply memorize the answer, which was identified as the "deductive" method. We also were required to learn about the history of education, both in Western countries as well as communist countries.

Psychology (especially child psychology), history, the arts, and culture were all emphasized. As mentioned in a previous chapter, singing of old Korean songs was discouraged due to their slow, inactive nature, whereas the school and party hierarchy encouraged the singing of more energetic songs. Translations of Russian songs were preferred and often performed at school concerts as well as other public gatherings. Music was emphasized at the teaching college. During my years there, I was in a singing group that often entered into contests. The instructor of the singing group was a talented violin player who played classical music. Ultimately the instructor became the leader of a North Korean band and achieved the rank of colonel.

The traditional lunar calendar was restored and included both the lunar Chusok date, as well as lunar new year holidays in addition to the Western solar calendar holidays.

Mathematics was also of importance, although since I was being trained for elementary through middle school education, my mathematics education extended only through higher algebra, trigonometry, and calculus. Schools enforced uniforms of white shirts and dark pants (or skirts for the girls). Boys typically wore white shirts, and girls wore sailor shirts. Both girls and boys would get additional stripes for their shirts to represent important projects completed. Middle schools also had uniforms in the quasi-military style of the Japanese. The dark blue coat of the school uniform usually had a number of badges on the front, signifying the school to which the wearer belonged, as well as any special awards that the wearer may have obtained. The strict requirements for collar inspection and gaiter seams matching pant seams were totally done away with.

As had been the case in the Japanese middle school, morning meetings were customary (morning "mass"). However, instead of being addressed by a school principal who read out the names of our classmates who had been accused of various misdemeanors by the police or attempted to indoctrinate us with a set of ethical principles via the periodic "su-shin" lecture, the meetings held under the North Korean principal generally consisted of the reading of various news articles from the paper, as well as routine exercise. Perhaps emboldened by the philosophy of the Russian occupiers, at one of these morning meetings, one of our student leaders (to my horror) took center stage to accuse the principal of collaborating too thoroughly with the Japanese in that he expelled various Korean students. The student told the principal to leave and never return, which he did the next day. (The principal was not really working as a principal but rather was working as a dean.) Luckily my father survived the "purges" that were occasioned by such "students" (probably agents of the party).

Although I was an outstanding student in school, one flaw in my education was my difficulty with English, in which I got a D one semester. Fortunately

I was able to find a tutor from among my friends. I taught my tutor Russian while my tutor taught me English. We met at my friend's house to study English even though his house was cold. The next semester I was able to pass English with a C. The presence of Russian guards had helped me learn Russian sufficiently well so that my friend was able to pass Russian.

In keeping with the government's desire to ensure prosperity and "fairness" for the inhabitants of its country, land reform also occurred, and as time went by progressed further under the North Korean government than under the Russians. Korean farmers produced in accordance with the Communist party dictates in amounts predetermined by the party under the various "five-year plans" that were promulgated by the party hierarchy. Farmers could keep a percentage of crops for personal food and sale at the local market, but the remainder was submitted to the government. This arrangement worked well in times of good weather, but in times of drought or bad weather, farmers sometimes had to buy crops at the market to provide to the government. However, a rationing system was in place that allowed farmers to be able to eat even in the worst of times.

In addition to land reform, the citizens of the country were expected to provide free labor to the government in order to accomplish a variety of social objectives. One prime objective was to eliminate illiteracy among the Korean public. Prior to WWII, about 30 percent of people were illiterate — mostly older people who had not had an opportunity to go through the Japanese educational system. It was made clear to all of those in the teacher's college that they would be expected to enlist not only themselves but their best students in an effort to eliminate illiteracy among the adults as part of the "free" labor provided in service to the state. Students were heavily propagandized to accept this, although no physical punishment was allowed in the school system against students. As during the Japanese occupation, students were responsible for cleaning their own schoolrooms. However, students were allowed to take their lunches to the playground to share their lunch toppings (fish, meat toppings, marinated vegetables) among their friends and not required to take lunch with the teachers. This was quite different than the arrangement under the Japanese, who required all lunches to be eaten in the presence of teachers.

Teachers had good salaries in North Korea and were expected to ensure good performance from their students on tests. They were rewarded if the class did well and punished if the class did poorly. (They may have been sent to a school in a rural area.) The final test of the year was given by the government. Independent, outside instructors were used during this most important test. Teachers were also responsible for the loyalty of students to the government.

In addition to assisting with adult education, however, more grueling labor was also expected of the grammar school students, usually in the form of construction brigades for dam, hospital, and farm projects. This provision of free labor was really a system of forced labor, with an income tax imposed in addition. Women were expected to perform as much physical labor as men, building hospitals, schools, and other government programs. If men were expected to dig up one bushel of gravel from the stream, then women also were expected to dig up one bushel of gravel. Free labor was expected of all able-bodied men and women during their winter and summer holidays, as well as on weekends and after work in accordance with the prevailing needs of the government and pursuant to the direction of the various party leaders. A coupon system was instituted to ensure that everyone participated in the public-works projects. Those unwilling to provide free labor would soon find themselves without a job or removed to the country, where they would likely have a lower-paying job and fewer resources than the city could provide.

When the North Korean government was permanently established, we found ourselves eating very cheap food. We had to eat yellow rice mixed with beans. The long-cherished Korean short-grained rice had become only a distant memory at this point, having first been consigned to the Japanese and now being unavailable to the Korean population for a variety of reasons. North Korean food sellers refused to pack down the rice container we brought to bring the rice home until they saw our money and had ensured that it was the right kind of money. Although the Russians had totally ruined the economy with their massive printing of bills, the North Koreans also continued with money exchanges, continually removing what little we had in the way of monetary reserves. Within a year and a half, the North Korean government had yet another monetary exchange. This totally removed all reserves from the house. Grandmother's savings from her apple stand were by this time totally gone, and we were living hand-to-mouth. Under the Japanese, there was at least stability to our finances. However, under the five-year economic plan, everything was unstable. Thus in addition to divesting the populace of its resources and savings, the government succeeded in making the populace almost entirely dependent upon the government for its livelihood and economic survival.

The five-year economic plan was imposed on all businesses. Pressures on all segments of the populace to meet the economic policy were very severe. The government decided to close its borders and not permit its people to trade with the outside world. They tried to ensure that they only consumed their own products, without reference to the outside world, and assured the populace that in the future their desires for consumer goods would be satisfied.

In its desire for "fairness," the North Korean government worked hard to eliminate corruption and bribery in the government. People who tried to bribe government officers were punished severely, along with the government officers who dared accept a bribe. Wrongdoers were made to stand on a public platform and confess their misdemeanors. Sanitation, especially in restaurants, was emphasized. Restaurant workers had to wear white clothes to work in order to emphasize the cleanliness of the restaurant, as well as the cleanliness of the server. If a restaurant was discovered to be unclean, the government would close the restaurant until the situation was corrected. The government tried to persuade people not to go to church, and ministers (Christian) were not allowed to preach sermons and were sent to jail for no reason. However, Buddhist monks were occasionally allowed to perform a ceremony in the interests of preserving historical traditions and norms, although I cannot recall ever seeing them with their classic begging bowls on the streets. Beggars on the street were captured and sent to a camp where they were fed and clothed and put to work for the government. Nevertheless, the traditional "mudang," or shamans, were allowed to ply their trade in ridding houses of evil spirits. I would walk past a mudang's house on my way to school on occasion, most often when we lived next to a mudang at one point. Mudang would sometimes tell their sick clients that they should put chicken meat or other sacrifices in a bamboo cage wrapped with cloth and hung from a lamp post. I would see these sacrificial offerings and when passing them would spit on the ground so as to ensure the ill luck would not follow me on my way to school. The mudang who lived next to my family paid a couple of visits to my mother when she was ill. Mudangs were not married as a rule; for some reason, most of them stayed single. Our neighborhood mudang's back yard was filled with debris, so she could locate healing items for her customers readily, and though she attempted to exorcise the evil spirits that were presumed to be taking my mother's life, it was to no avail. One day when an especially lively ceremony was being conducted, Youngchan, my sister, Heechan, and I, as well as my maternal grandmother, decided to get a better look from the vantage point of the roof of the tool shed. Unfortunately our combined weights caused the roof of the shed to collapse, sending us into the interior. Fortunately nobody was hurt in the collapse.

Another time a mudang had attempted to exorcise the ghost of someone thought to have died in a house that my father had purchased and was attempting to renovate. (The sound of someone washing dishes could be heard clearly at night, and upon excavating the kitchen floor, human bones were discovered.) Despite the mudang's attempts, the ghostly dishwasher could still be heard. Father, believing that the house contained an unquiet spirit, had moved his family elsewhere as quickly as he could. Whenever I would see the brightly colored ribbons and ornaments festooning the trees and telephone poles, I would recognize that the mudang was in the process of conducting an exorcism or house cleansing to rid the house of evil spirits. Sometimes ceremonies (which involved chanting and a Korean gong, as well as dancing atop vertical sword blades with bare feet) would last for as much as three days, usually from two to four in the afternoon. The purpose of the ceremonies was to drive away the evil spirits that were thought to be afflicting a sick person, who need not be present for the ceremony. Mudang would often put brightly colored clothes in a basket with eggs as a show of force against the evil spirits who would try to possess a house or a person. Objects that were in the house of a dying person would often be destroyed or given away so as to remove the jinx between the dead person and his possessions. Mudang in Japanese is known as "miko." I once had a Hungarian friend by the last name of Miko. He believed that one of his ancestors had been a mudang!

Koreans have somewhat of a tradition of being animists — that is, people who believe in individual spirits inhabiting different types of substance. For example, cats have long been viewed as evil creatures in an otherworldly sense, and trees, rivers, flowers, houses, and animals all have their unique spirits. Common articles, such as books, are believed to have their own unique spirits, which must be respected. For example, it was believed that books should never be placed on the floor or handled carelessly. Rather they should be placed reverently on a table and used in a respectful manner. And of course such beliefs can lead to raw superstition. For example, much was made of the fact that the Beijing Olympics were occurring on 8/8/88, the number 8 being a number of great power and fortuity. This caused me to recall that a very fortunate, prosperous person was termed "pahl-tsa"; the Chinese word for "eight" is "pahl."

Communist indoctrination meetings took up much of the ordinary person's time and created much resentment. Typically it was connected with the person's place of employment, although there were block monitors assigned to each of the city blocks in Pyongyang. The indoctrination meetings might last for five or more hours in the evening. Communist Party members pronounced their opinions on the efforts of the worker's efforts within the workplace.

The North Korean Communist Party required that its members, as well as members of the family, not be former white-collar workers who were previously engaged in the managerial aspects of business. Their belief was that white-collar workers were unfit for manual labor and would be unsuitable party members, being naturally soft. The former low-wage workers were the ideal candidates for the party but were of dubious ability when it came to making decisions for important social institutions. My father's former status under the Japanese disqualified him and the rest of the family from being members in the Communist Party. Janitors and manual laborers became the new members of the Communist Party — and hence part of the new elite. They became the leaders of the factories, offices, and other important organizations.

Movements of the populace were controlled also. People could not readily quit their job and move elsewhere, as the government controlled access to both housing and jobs. People had to get official permission to move from one town to another. Under the North Korean system, most people had jobs, usually what the government had assigned to the person. People who were cooperative with the government and who did what they were told were usually assigned to work in the city under desirable conditions. They could not freely change their jobs, however. If they lost their government-assigned job, they could not usually find another one very readily.

This social revolution, which inverted the social structure, created much grumbling throughout the country, though no one spoke too loudly, being afraid of being sent to Siberia. Communists responded that persons who grumbled in this manner were really bloodsuckers who had been previously living off the efforts of others very unfairly. Party members were responsible for leading important meetings and providing authority for government activities. Some were silent members and informed on other members of the community.

The implementation of a highly effective spy system, together with the indoctrination of the populace in the theory and tenets of Marxism, and their ability to control the schools, government, and the armed forces is the reason that the 5 percent of the population that was convinced of the truth and necessity of the Communist cause was able to control the 95 percent of the populace that was discontent with the way things were progressing. Votes were not free. Communists spied on voters to ensure votes went to the right box. The army, which often acts as a conservative force in the face of unproven and irrational government objectives, was maintained largely by conscripts who were typically placed in the frontlines. Most soldiers were drafted and unwilling to fight. If troops tried to retreat, they were shot by the Communist rear guard.

The face of Premier Kim Il-Sung glowered down at the population from most public places, usually accompanied by a portrait of Stalin or Lenin. His reference as "General Kim" was most peculiar since his last army rank was lieutenant in the Korean Army. He would have to have had a great many field promotions during his time as a guerrilla fighting the Japanese in order to have achieved the rank of general. Nevertheless, a number of songs were dedicated to Kim Il-Sung, Stalin, and Moscow.

The totalitarian face of government in North Korea made anti-Western propaganda very prominent. Western countries were regarded as evil and promoting colonialism throughout the world. People who had worked for Japanese and who had made a lot of money were regarded as traitors. The North Koreans viewed South Koreans as traitors for cooperating with the U.S., selling the country to the aggressor. All of Southeast Asia had fallen to the Western powers, and the only countries left uncolonized were Korea, China, and Japan. The saga of how Hong Kong was conquered by Western religion in the face of the Ming Dynasty was emphasized. The Chinese had traditionally never had an organized army — only warriors in the service of various warlords and the emperor. The Christian missionaries were viewed as the advance troops for those governments, which hoped that the Chinese peasants would have an uprising against the Chinese rulers. An example that the North Korean

government cited was contained in the book *Keys to the Kingdom*, which described the life of a missionary who tried to advocate for the peasants in the
face of pressure to create an uprising against the dynasty. The priest was called
back to his main religious house and told to not do so much work to help the
Chinese people but rather to create an uprising against the Chinese government. He refused to do so and was relieved of his mission.

Another unsavory tactic often cited was the effort of the British to addict
the Chinese to opium collected from India, Burma, Malaysia, and other nearby
countries. One morning a Chinese warrior discovered that an opium ship was
to be unloaded and, in company with about twenty other warriors, burned it
instead. As a result, the Chinese government had to open all the port cities in
the Chinto Peninsula and give Hong Kong to Britain under a hundred-year
lease. Prominent was Chinto Island, which was opened to Japanese and European powers (the British, Germans, and others). These examples of Western
interference were meant to convince the Korean people that Westerners were
uniformly evil and incapable of being trusted.

Educational System in North Korea

The North Korean educational system was comparable in many ways to that
instituted by the Japanese occupation, except that it emphasized Marxism,
Leninism, and Stalinism in ways that would be useful to the government. No
physical punishment was allowed in the school, unlike the system under the
Japanese. Instead control of the students using persuasion, peer influence, and
indoctrination was emphasized. Political science was introduced at the earliest
school grade and increased in emphasis until graduation from high school. All
subjects, including music, language, history, science, and mathematics, were
reorganized and re-presented to include the proper political (Communist) view
of the subject. Music from the great Russian revolution was emphasized, and
new songs which praised the great Kim Il-Sung, the Russians, and the revolution were created and sung. Language classes were an ideal opportunity to
read the Communist works in the native Korean language. (Of course the common language of the Orient, which had utilized Chinese characters, was allowed to fall into disuse, being deemed as a vestige of the hated Japanese.)
Korean history was brought back from the memories of the old people, and
the few remaining old, Korean history books, which had managed to escape

the book burnings of the Japanese, once again saw the light of day. Science and mathematics were also retooled in the service of the ideology.

Evolution was one primary topic that was emphasized to demonstrate the "rational" freedom from religion under the Communist ideology. The instructors talked a great deal about evolution of earth and how humans evolved from primal matter, emphasizing that human beings are not created by God. They emphasized that the use of tools, such as sticks in order to get apples from the apple tree, caused the evolution and progression of man, in that the ape-man had to both stand up to achieve his goals and learn to use tools. While the Stone Age introduced the first tools, it was still necessary to fool or intimidate one's neighbors in order to get enough to eat. With increasing competition for resources, the Age of Slavery came about, making it more profitable to enslave one's neighbors rather than kill them. Religion was useful in quelling or forestalling slave uprisings, in that the masters were able to fool the slaves with promises of a better afterlife by using religion. As the plantations and manors gave way to cities and towns, great nations arose. The feudal nation-states rewarded their defenders with land and money in order to keep away outsiders and maintain social stability at home. This was the introduction of the "totalitarian" age. This phase lasted until the introduction of the capitalistic society, which emphasized free trade among nations at the expense of individual workers and required the looting of resources, both overseas and in disadvantaged areas of the nation. While the capitalistic society lasted, it was good for the capitalists, but the store of colonies that could absorb excess population — and from which natural resources could be stolen — was quickly exhausted. Then came the imperialistic society, which sought to extend national influence by means of theft of colonies from other countries. This lasted until after WWII, when the colonies revolted against their masters. It was noted that the time frames during which each of these types of governments operated kept getting shorter and shorter. Gradually socialism was introduced. ("From each according to his abilities, to each according to his needs.") Socialism was working toward communism, the utopian structure. Under the utopian structure, one could work and attain his desires, which would be granted by the government in accordance with the contribution to society under communism. Although the North Korean government made no pretense to offering a "utopia," this was the stated future objective of the government.

According to communist theory, human life and its progression was dictated by the environment, with the child being born "tabula rasa." A gentle child would be made gentle by his parents. Conversely a mean child would be made mean by his parents. All people are products of their environment, according to the communist theory, with moral choices often severely circumscribed in accordance with their early education. Those acting "inappropriately" would require "re-education." The concept of spiritual development does not make much headway under the communist view of things, as the spiritual life makes one master of his own destiny and moral choices, without reference to material circumstances.

The teaching of mathematics was also suborned into the service of the DPRK. Below is an excerpt from a paper I wrote after coming to the U.S. and which describes the insinuation of political principles into the subject of mathematics (otherwise viewed as operating in the objective realm) without reference to subjective influences:

Teaching of Math in North Korea (Principles of Elementary School Mathematics Education in Communist Countries)

This paper explains mainly the objectives, methods, and application of the teaching of elementary school mathematics in communist nations. Although this article explains mathematical teaching principles of elementary schools in North Korea, the overall concepts of mathematical education among the communist countries are basically the same.

The primary purpose of mathematics education in a communist nation is identical to that of any non-communist nation: To acquire pupils with numerical systems and their application in their daily lives. This objective is also aimed to develop pupils' mental capacities for solving mathematical problems rapidly and accurately.

The secondary purpose of teaching mathematics in communist schools is more important than the primary purpose of the above paragraph. This is to induce pupils to be loyal to their present form of government. Many mathematical problems of school textbooks are written such that the pupils can compare the economic outputs of their government with those of other capitalistic countries, whether the actual figures are realistic or not. Under such an education system, the pupils, including the first grade children, will be proud of their economic structure.

In order to achieve the above objectives, the government insists on including the mathematical problems in textbooks, as is illustrated in the following example of a third grade problem.

"During the Japanese Occupation in Korea, a worker produced 10 pairs of shoes per day and earned 15 yen a day. During the administration of the People's Republic of Korea, the same worker produced 15 pairs of shoes per day and earned 30 yen per day. What is the increased daily production in percent that he produced under the new government, and how much more did he earn per shoe during that period?"

Along with the problem solving, the teacher must conclude the class with the following typical statement:

"The worker produced less quantity of shoes during Japanese occupation because of the poor and inefficient working conditions. However, with the improved working conditions under the Communist government, he is able to produce more shoes, and his earning and living conditions are better than before. If it had not been for the help of the great Russian army, the worker would have lived poor forever."

The method used to conduct mathematics class was classified as a "semi-inductive" method. In the classroom, the teacher assists pupils to arrive at the solutions for solving equations or problems. However, the teacher tends to lead the pupils to solve the problems in his or her ways. If there is any alternative solution raised from any pupil, the teacher upgrades the solution and admires the pupil for such achievement, but the teacher eventually leads the pupils to accept the teacher's solution. The deductive method was seldom used in North Korea.

Each teacher must prepare his lecture in written form at least a semester prior to the following semester when the subjects will be taught. Each written form must be prepared in detail, including descriptions about anticipated questions. The following is a typical outline of the lecture form:

1. Subject, Teaching Date, Approval
2. Brief description of subject and the area of coverage
3. Purposes of teaching the subject in connection with the principles of government
4. Visual aid materials for subject, if any. (Most of the visual aids were posters made or drawn by teachers.)

5.   Review of assignments and previous lessons (fifteen minutes)
6.   Discussion of today's subject (twenty-five minutes)
7.   Review and summary of today's subject (five minutes)
8.   Assignment (five minutes)
     The assignments are usually selected in the following proportions, which can be classified in the "semi-oblique method."
     a.   Problems from previous lessons that relate to today's subject (20 percent)
     b.   Problems from today's subject (60 percent)
     c.   Problems to be learned in the following class period (20 percent)
     Particularly for a third grade pupil, the average time he or she spends to complete the assignment is 1½ hours to 2 hours every other day during the week. This is approximately 30 percent of the total time he or she spends for entire assignments of various subjects.

While I was a teacher, I gave intermediate quizzes on an average of once every two weeks. Final examinations were usually prepared and given by the government with the supervision of the board of education. If the results of the tests were not satisfactory, the teacher would be on probation for a year or would be terminated. Teachers in North Korea were highly respected and well-paid; however, they were responsible for the pupils' scholastic achievements and disciplinary problems, as well as the individual student's loyalties to the government.

As can be seen by the foregoing, the primary purpose of math in North Korea was to provide enhanced intelligence and problem-solving skills, although the political agenda of the DPRK was also made highly apparent via word problems. There were times when I silently rebelled against my function as a mouthpiece for the government, though I dared not speak of it. The method of allowing the students to reach reasoned conclusions to stated problems was called the semi-inductive method. The deductive method, which depended upon rote memorization, was seldom used in North Korea, except for certain areas such as the memorization of multiplication tables, as well as the primary Marxist-Leninist principles that divided North Korea from the rest of the non-communist world.

Fortunately there were a number of areas that still permitted me to be creative and enjoy the use of my innate faculties without having to concern myself with the political correctness of my activities. Although my free time was largely consumed with "free labor" activities, not all of it involved manual labor. As a prospective teacher, I was expected to lead other students in my middle school, as well as our prospective elementary school students, in various political activities, some of which involved the support of military activities, including parades and the hosting of dignitaries. As such I was sometimes called to paint rousing pictures to incite revolutionary fervor. My paint was bought from a paint store, not an art shop. I painted a variety of things, notably the memorial near my home that celebrated the Russian occupation of Korea, as well as Stalin's portrait and Kim Il-Sung's portrait. Additionally I was expected to assist in ensuring that students would be ready with their marching routines in preparation for the military parades that were a frequent occurrence in the early days of the DPRK. Military influences abounded, and parades with military regiments were frequent.

May Day parades were important, as was the Korean Liberation Day in August and the October Revolution anniversary for Russia. Students had to practice marching weeks prior to the parades. Parades typically began at the city square with everyone standing — no chairs were available. Chants to Kim Il-Sung and Stalin were expected, especially by the members of the Young Man's Association.

After the verbal salutes, Kim Il-Sung would appear on the balcony of city hall. At first he didn't speak Korean very well, but later he improved greatly. His speeches were typically long-winded and addressed such things as the current five-year economic plan. After the speech was over, the parade would begin. New military hardware would be displayed, and then the soldiers would pass by. Under the hot sun, some people would faint while standing at attention. After the speech was over, a variety of labor organizations, schools, and others would march by, often carrying posters or banners to show for inspection and saluting Kim Il-Sung. I was responsible for painting some of the posters that were displayed in those parades.

I also painted a variety of landscapes. I invited a friend, Inkun Choi, who was about seven years older than I and married with one daughter, to my home. He was an excellent painter, and together we painted the surroundings of the city water area. Inkun Choi sometimes invited me for a meal at his house. He was well-read in philosophy and was a kind man. I treated him as a big brother.

During my last two years at teacher's college, I was approached by the school administrator, who asked me to teach a variety of high school subjects, including art and calculus, as a substitute or student teacher. This experience nearly ended in disaster, though had I been older, I would have undoubtedly been wiser. My students were a class of girls (high school sophomores), and everyone got along very well, or so I thought at the time. The girls thought I was a cute, little devil, which probably made me less than cautious. I immediately noticed one very beautiful girl in the class, Rhee Suk-za, and proceeded to write her a page and a half letter, noting her admirable traits, though omitting the word "love." I folded it origami-style and gave it to the class leader and asked her to deliver it to Miss Rhee, never dreaming she would open it. In the next couple of days, everyone knew of the letter that I had written to Miss Rhee. I was appalled that the class leader had read my letter, though we never spoke of it. The following day the associate dean of the school called me into his office and cautioned me against pursuing a relationship with Miss Rhee. He indicated that I was on probation over the matter and warned me to be careful.

I talked to my friend Ingun Choi about the matter and persuaded him to talk to her about me. A few weeks later, Choi talked to Miss Rhee. He said that she had complained about the letter I had written and the commotion it had caused. ("Why didn't he talk to me directly rather than write a letter that got out to everyone?") Relations afterward were a trifle strained from there on out. In my final year, I was required to take a final exam that covered all the subjects I had covered in teacher's college (history of education, psychology, mathematics, etc.). Not only was a written exam required but also an oral exam. I studied very hard — until midnight on most evenings after I had completed my work on the public-works projects. My failure with Miss Rhee spurred my efforts to pass my exams with high honors. There were a variety of examiners, including members of the Communist party, as well as some of my former teachers, and it lasted for about a week. I knew after I had completed the examinations that I had done well but had no idea as to how well I had done.

At the graduation ceremony, the principal called my name and asked me to step forward. My father was not there due to the pressures of work, and besides, he tended to view school activities as being relatively unimportant. Other

important members of the community (including parents) were there, however, as well as the lower classmen. Miss Rhee was there, as was her mother.
Her father was a medical doctor, and her mother was a member of the PTA
and a wealthy and prominent member of the community.

My certificate of high honors was provided by the vice premier of North
Korea. Another certificate was given by the education board in North Korea.
Only three students in North Korea received that type of honor. With tears
streaming down my face, I descended the podium, wishing my own dead mother
could have seen me. My father was only mildly interested to see the certificates,
saying "It's good you have made good grades." Inside I am sure that my father
was very pleased, but it was not considered proper at that time to show too much
enthusiasm for special awards. The certificate went with my sister when she went
to my aunt's house to carry photographs and other mementos.

I had a choice of any school I wanted to teach in. I finally decided to teach
at the grammar school in the teacher's college, which was used mainly to train
the seniors at the teacher's college as student teachers. I started teaching second
grade, but the parents asked me to continue teaching the same class, which
meant I taught third grade — until the war started.

My Teaching Experience in North Korea (Fall 1948 – Summer 1950)

As a teacher, I was expected to embrace the increasingly rigid philosophy of
the North Korean educational system. Although it had begun by patterning
itself on the Russian educational system, it treated some subjects in more
depth, and despite its resistance to the deductive method of education, which
emphasized rote memorization, the North Korean government emphasized
the memorization of the principles of Stalinism, Leninism, and anti-American
and anti-Japanese doctrine.

Due to my excellent grades and the award at my graduation ceremony from
teacher's college, I had been selected to go to Moscow for further training. Out
of all Pyongyang, only twelve persons would be selected for such an honor.
However, due to my father's earlier position as a white-collar worker under the
Japanese, I was blocked from going to Moscow, as the Communist Party believed I might be unfit to participate. Instead a young man who was a much
worse student but who was active in the Young Man's Association was selected
to go to Moscow. My father was sympathetic but told me that it probably would

be better for my future to not go to Moscow, perhaps sensing that I would one day eventually go to the U.S. and leave North Korea behind, as he had once encouraged me to do during my school days under the Japanese.

Needless to say, I was somewhat ambivalent about my role in the North Korean educational system. A teacher's responsibilities in those days included the brainwashing of the students as to how wonderful the Communist government under Kim Il-Sung was. I was responsible for teaching math in the classroom and often held open sessions for inspection, which would be attended by local leaders of the Communist Party. I was also responsible for physical education of the entire school and led aerobic exercises for the students at the morning mass. I also wrote reading, writing, math, art, and Korean textbooks that were used by schools throughout North Korea.

In addition I was responsible for making visual aids and posters for classroom use during the summer vacation, which usually lasted for about one month. The posters were usually made of water-soluble paint media (tempera), with old posters used in the classroom needing to be replaced each semester. Typically posters dealt with anti-American and anti-Japanese themes. One particularly memorable poster dealt with Uncle Sam chaining the necks of South Korean politicians and Third World peoples, who were carrying bags of dollars on their backs. During the summer, teachers were required to attend meetings in educational theory, as well as political-education classes in Marxism. They were also expected to grade homework books weekly during the summer, in addition to writing the next semester's lesson plans.

Despite my reservations, I enjoyed my teaching at the local grammar school that adjoined the teacher's college from which I had matriculated. I was then nineteen years of age. My responsibility was to teach at the middle school, as well as to instruct seniors at the teacher's college as to how best to improve their teaching methods in preparation for their graduation.

The grammar school shared a playground with the teacher's college, and the buildings were brick with wooden floors. My friend Choi was also selected to teach at the same school. I selected a girl's class (second grade, eight years old) while Choi was selected to teach the boy's class at the same class level. The girl's class and Korean school were located at one end of the compound; at the other end was a block of Russian families, mostly Russian soldiers with families. I was able to speak Russian, so I was sometimes invited for lunch at the Russian compound. The school itself had about a thousand students, both boys and girls. Each grade had about four different classes: two classes of girls, two classes of boys.

Most class sizes ranged from sixty-five to seventy students. I enjoyed my relationship with both the students and their parents. Ensuring student success was largely the result of cooperation with parents. In my class were three or four daughters of government ministers, as well as three or four daughters of wealthy people. One of them was the daughter of the paint store owner, who was heavily involved with the PTA. Another of my class students was the younger sister of Miss Rhee (to whom I had written the ill-advised letter), and her mother was very active in the PTA. It appeared that Miss Rhee Sup-za was attending teaching college as well.

I tried to make the school day as pleasant as possible for my pupils. In those days, there was about a ten- to fifteen-minute rest period between each class. During those rest periods, I sometimes played the organ in a rather haphazard manner, practicing some simple North Korean songs, and would sometimes be joined by my pupils in singing them. After the rest period, the children were expected to resume their seats immediately and conduct themselves in a respectful manner. In the rare case of encountering a disobedient student, I seldom inflicted physical punishment but rather set the offending student to stand outside on the playground or required her to clean the classroom twice in a row. As under the Japanese school system, classrooms were still expected to be cleaned by pupils and inspected by teachers.

One exception to the no-physical-punishment rule was a time when I had taken over a class for my friend Choi in reading and writing. One of the kids made a racket, and I knuckled his head. Unbeknownst to me, the child had scabs on his head, which the knuckling removed, causing his scalp to bleed. I took my handkerchief from my pocket and absorbed as much blood as possible. The student assured me that he would not report the incident to his father, who was an important figure in the North Korean government. From that day forward, I tried to be as circumspect as possible about delivering any type of punishment.

My salary was three hundred won, considered a relatively good one, and was supplemented with cloth and food rations. Still our family was relatively poor, considering its earlier status under the Japanese occupation. I was expected to work much harder than the normal worker and take the leading role in civic projects, as well as ensuring the progress of my pupils. Due to my young age, I was still considered a baby teacher, as I still taught school in my school uniform — largely because I couldn't afford new clothes. The cloth I received as part of my wages went to make my father's clothes, and my paycheck went to help provide for the entire family.

Teachers were expected to make a lesson plan for the entire year, which had to be approved by a member of the Communist Party to ensure that nothing would be said against the government. Revisions to the plan had to be approved three days prior to the lecture, including responses to be provided in anticipation of student questions. Each lesson plan had at least six pages that were required to be filled in. Typically there were forty lesson plans per subject. This was sometimes difficult, in that there was only a month vacation in the summer.

All lecture plans were reviewed and revised periodically. If not satisfactory to the Communist Party, the lecture plan needed to be revised at least three days prior.

One of the highlights in the class was addition and subtraction of two-digit numbers without benefit of pencil and paper. This was a most popular form of mental exercise with the kids and allowed them to display their skills.

One of the important features of the school was the self-criticism of teachers, who would report on their daily activities, cite the difficulties encountered, and relate the achievement that their students had made. They also had to outline the objectives they hoped to attain during the upcoming week. The teachers had to recite their faults to their fellow teachers, identifying their shortcomings in punishing the students or failure to teach the students. Sometimes such meetings would go on until 9:30 or 10:00 P.M., with the teachers still being expected to come to school no later than 8 A.M. the next day. After enumerating the week's activities and assessing the progress of my students against the planned objectives, I myself would usually own up to such faults as being too severe with the students, which "confession" was usually taken in good part.

Out of the thirty teachers at the school, one or two were members of the Communist Party, and one or two were members of the secret police. Most meetings of teachers (including the school principal and dean of the school) were led by members of the Communist Party. One of the key thoughts of the Communist teachers was that students should be more devoted to the school and government and spend more time for the school and civic work projects rather than the family. This meant that the school day was lengthened from 2 P.M. to 3 P.M.

The main free-labor project that teachers were asked to do was collect taxes from illiterate taxpayers, as well as to school them such that they would be able to read and write. Also teachers were responsible for making propaganda speeches to labor organizations and for leading students to help teach illiterate adults. This effort also consumed most of the free time of my best students, who were also struggling to keep up their grades, make political speeches at election time, assist in tax collection, and meet other family expectations. This was true even for second grade students, who were each responsible for teaching five to ten illiterate adults, although lesson plans would be the responsibility of the teacher. Failure of illiterate adults to pass the examinations prepared by the government in reading and writing would be the responsibility of the cognizant teacher. About 15 to 20 percent of older adults had no knowledge of reading and writing. Since many older adults were also not fluent in speaking Korean (having been raised under Japanese auspices), it was doubly difficult for them to learn to read and write Korean.

Teachers would also be responsible for ensuring the success of any local government construction project by supervising the efforts of the community, which was expected to provide free labor for building hospitals, schools, or government buildings. Teachers were expected to work alongside the workers digging gravel or whatever and not just supervise.

As the war approached during the first part of 1950, I was asked to supervise a night workforce to bury the upper portion of the Tadong River. The Americans had bombed all the bridges that crossed the Tadong River, and the city had ordered the civilians to bury the river from either side of the river using gravel. (This was to enable tanks to cross the river.) It was very narrow and was easy to bury. The upper stream was so pure that it was used for the city water. The city water island was near the upper stream. The civilians were asked to bring all their own tools (shovels, picks, rakes) and work at night. Sometimes they worked with a light, sometimes without depending on whether there were American search planes flying. The civilians on either side of the river worked to fill the river in with gravel. The tanks were able to cross a wooden bridge that had been placed on top of the gravel. This project required twenty nights of forced labor. Some civilians fell asleep near the gravel pits; I tried to keep them awake if a member of the Communist Party was in the vicinity. The project effort usually ended at about 4:30 in the morning. I had about a forty-minute walk home, crossing the bridge to the city water area. By the time I got home, my father would usually be cooking breakfast, often a dish of chicken marinated in soy sauce.

After breakfast I still had to go to school and teach, perhaps one hour later than usual, with another teacher substituting for me. There was no rest for teachers during the beginning of the war. At least once a year, students or instructors from the teacher's college would come over to take over the instruction for about two months, which would enable me to rest at the rear of the classroom while evaluating the substitute teachers.

During the years just prior to the war, as well as during the period of time when the war had just begun, teachers were also expected to watch the school building at night. I was fortunate that on those long evenings, the parents would send suppers through their children. Once Mrs. Rhee sent a particularly delicious supper through her daughter. There was no question of bribery or favoritism, however, in that each child's parents took turns providing the teacher's supper. The children would typically take that opportunity to get additional instruction on problems that they had encountered in the classroom earlier in the week. Male teachers had one personal room, and female teachers had one personal room for use on those nights while they were on guard duty. On one night when the women's rooms were unheated, they came to sleep in the men's room. Although nothing romantic happened, it caused some awkward moments. There was one other incident that occurred during this most painful period of my life prior to arrival in South Korea as a refugee. During the winter vacation of 1949, I needed to update a lesson plan at school. I had to go to school to do this. Upon arriving at school, I encountered a janitor, who was cleaning the room. The janitor was about fifty with salt and pepper hair. He collapsed, foaming at the mouth and making strange noises. Fortunately I managed to summon the help of two other teachers who were also at the school watching it. From his behavior, we determined that he had epilepsy. We transported him to the doctor, who was Miss Rhee's father. He counseled us to put chopsticks in his mouth to prevent him from swallowing his tongue and to wait twenty minutes. Sure enough, after twenty minutes the janitor came around and recovered consciousness.

I required students who made good grades to help tutor their own classmates. My class usually made more progress than the other classes at the same grade level in the school. Despite my rigid expectations, parents often asked the school principal to allow me to teach advanced-level classes and ensure that their children would be placed in my class.

A PTA meeting indicated that additional funds were needed for the school. A collection taken up by the parents for the classroom yielded five thousand won; a few days later a separate contribution of three hundred won was provided, collected from the parents. Unbeknownst to me, the three hundred won was meant for me alone; I turned it in nevertheless. The school principal was very impressed, as I had collected more than any other teacher. About a week later, the mother of Miss Rhee approached me and told me that the parents had given the three hundred won as a gift to me alone in thanks for my good performance with the kids. I thanked her and told her that I felt better about turning in the entire amount. Although our family could have used the money, I would not dare take it, especially in light of the heavy penalties that were imposed for bribery and favoritism under the North Korean government.

I was often invited to dine with the parents of my students. Despite the parents' assurances that they were giving me only a very small amount of liquor, I sometimes poured the liquor into a separate glass under the table due to my sensitivity to it. Once at a dinner with parents, before I realized what was happening, I got drunk and vomited in the streetcar. I managed to sneak into the complex past the Russian guard through the bedroom window and get to bed without creating a disturbance. Fortunately my father did not discover the fact that I had crept in late at night drunk. Although my father drank heavily at times, he was not pleased at the prospect of his children's drinking, and I did not want to make an issue of it with my father. So I continued to pretend to drink at the parents' dinners while pouring the liquor in a separate bowl and blotting it up with my Kleenex.

At the end of my first year of teaching, all my students were promoted to third grade without failure. Unfortunately in the next year, there were three students who failed to pass onto fourth grade (in 1950, the year when the war started). The parents were most anxious to learn what had gone wrong in order to prevent a repetition of the failure. One girl who had failed to come to class four days in a row was a source of concern; her mother came to visit me about the situation and revealed that the girl's father was dead and that the mother had argued with the daughter previously. The mother asked me to punish the girl for not attending school and for not coming home. The lack of a good family life was as important to Korean kids as it is to any other children.

One young man (Baek) came onto the teaching staff at the middle school where I taught as a geography instructor. He had been a POW in Hamung in the northeast section of Korea and had been sent there due to his efforts to destabilize the Japanese regime. He was caught by the Korean police and put in a cell with a filthy latrine that was smelly and dank. The guards would periodically spray the entire cell with a fire hose and spray Baek's body with the high-pressure water. He feigned insanity by eating his own excrement and was finally released by the Japanese warden. He changed his identity and found his way to a private college (which was originally established by U.S. missionaries), where he resumed his teacher's training. When the Japanese started to close the colleges to recruit the inhabitants to the Japanese war effort, he found his way into a Korean naval detachment as a supply clerk. His ship went down in the South Pacific, torpedoed by the Americans. He was left to survive on a wooden door that had detached itself from the ship, skimming the surface of the ocean. He spent four days on the ocean. On the third day, due to dehydration and lack of food, he was incoherent, dreaming he was in a field of flowers and hearing his mother's voice repeatedly telling him to get up. When he woke up, he found that he was still on the ocean, the sparkling water seeming to resemble a bed of flowers. He went to sleep again but was awoken by the sound of an approaching U.S. naval ship. He was picked up by the U.S. Navy and saved from death.

Although he was originally sent to a POW camp in Taiwan, he was eventually spotted as a potentially useful person to the U.S. war effort. He spent some time in a Hawaiian prison camp trying to persuade the Japanese prisoners of war of the rightness of the U.S. cause.

When the war ended, Baek returned to Japan along with other Koreans who had been in the naval detachment that had been supporting the Japanese war effort. However, the Koreans in Japan were not treated well there, so he eventually elected to return to North Korea and resume his contact with his guerrilla friends whom had had met during his stay in the Japanese prison camp. The rest of his detachment chose to go to South Korea. His experiences and acquaintances had left him with definite pro-Communist leanings, which I could appreciate but could not share.

One evening I was studying outside of the house overlooking the park near the water tanks. The quietness of the surroundings was helpful in study, and my siblings came up to join me as it was getting dark. Although nothing had been said about the possibility of my departure from North Korea, we fell into conversation about how best to be faithful to our family, especially our stepmother, and to visit our mother's grave. I recall that my brother Inchon, who was a leader in his fifth grade class, wore a shirt covered with badges and stripes, signifying his leadership rank. They all agreed to try to visit Mother's grave every year at Chusok, whether or not I was around.

Toward the end of my second year of teaching, I was invited to the home of the North Korean minister of economy, as his daughter was in my class. I was at the man's home until quite late, waiting for him to return. Although the minister's wife greeted me, her husband did not return to his home until about 10 P.M., having been in a meeting with Kim Il-Sung. Although the man had an important position in the North Korean government, the minister and his wife appeared to live in rather straitened circumstances judging by the appearance of the house and its contents. His child often came to school with torn shoes and stockings and looked otherwise unkempt. It was very obvious that at that time, the North Korean politicians did not live the privileged life that some believe they now enjoy under Kim Jong-un. When the minister returned, he apologized for keeping me waiting but explained that he had had a meeting with Kim Il-Sung that could not be delayed. The minister and I spent some time talking about his job and the pressures that he was under before I finally was able to leave for my own home in the city water compound. Unfortunately two days later, the North Korean minister's house that I had visited was bombed, with no indication as to whether the occupants survived. The entire school was closed the next day.

The American bombing of the Pyongyang area brought my teaching career to an end. The bombing was originally toward only military targets, but later the bombing included civilian targets. During the beginning of the Korean War, the entire school complex was bombed by American bombers.

After the school was bombed, the government closed it, and I occasionally went to school to ensure it was not being further damaged or looted, but there was no more classroom teaching. However, it enabled me to come to the U.S. for the second portion of my career, this time as an engineer.

Endnotes
1. Max Hastings, *The Korean War* (New York: Simon & Schuster, 1987), 37-43.
2. David Halberstam, *The Coldest Winter* (New York: Hyperion, 2007), 74.

Chapter VII
The Korean War Begins

*L*ife in Korea during Korean War
The Korean War lasted three years, beginning in June 1950 and ending in July 1953. The total combined casualties were 33,629 Americans killed and 105,785 wounded; the South Korean army lost 415,000 with 429,000 wounded. The Commonwealth (Britain, Canada, Australia, and New Zealand) lost 1,263 with 4,817 wounded. Belgium, Colombia, Ethiopia, France, Greece, Holland, the Philippines, Thailand, and Turkey lost 1,800 among them with 7,000 wounded.[1] People died from both bombing and ideology. North Korean troops went after non-Communists in the North, and in South Korea, the South Korean Army went after Communists. The South Korean Army went after Communists in North Korea as well during the time that South Korea invaded it. War atrocities were common with people being burned alive in their houses over ideology. In many cases, the armed forces had nothing to do with the killing. It was civilians killing civilians.

The Korean War was the result of conflicts between two large nations: the U.S. and the Soviet Union. Both sides were puppets of their respective ideologies. The Soviets wanted to take over the whole Korean peninsula, as well as Japan, and ultimately establish their rule over all Asia and block all American influence. The Soviets supplied air force planes, set up the Communist government, and engaged in troop training in North Korea. Conversely the U.S. tried to bomb the hydraulic power plant on the Yalu River and deprive Pyongyang and the North Korean industrial base of its chief energy supply, as well as its clean mountain water.

June 25, 1950, was the actual date the Korean War started. I had just completed two years of teaching school at Pyongyang Normal School and was getting ready for my third year of teaching there. As the school was on summer vacation, I was sent by the school principal to another local school facility to take two weeks of gymnastics training in order to take over the position of athletic director in the Pyongyang Normal school in addition to my regular teaching responsibilities. The classroom was in the indoor gym on the third floor of the school. The instructor, Mr. Yunn, was a young Korean about thirty-five years old who had just returned from Moscow, where he had received training through the Russian Athletic Institute. He was responsible for all gym instruction in the city of Pyongyang. He was full of praise for the Soviet system, including the air transport system. Parallel bars, horse, tumbling, and high bars were all part of the training, and the local school where I was to train was one of the few schools in the city that had an indoor gym.

By the end of the first week of training, I was able to perform somersaults over the wooden horse stand with a great deal of ease. I was practicing on the horse stand along with the other fifteen gym teachers from other schools in Pyongyang when Mr. Yunn told everyone to stop. Mr. Yunn informed everyone that the war had just started at the 38th parallel line on the west coast of the Korean peninsula. The instructor then turned on the radio, where the beginnings of the war were detailed. The radio said that South Korean troops had begun attacking at the border at 4 A.M. and that the North Koreans soldiers began to counterattack. The only radio station that the public was permitted to listen was the nationally operated broadcasting station, so there was no chance of switching stations to verify the information. All radio stations broadcasting from South Korea or Japan had been jammed by the government. The instructor assured everyone present that North Korea would soon be attacking deep inside South Korea and that the South Koreans would soon be liberated from their imperialistic society.

The revelation of the actual beginnings of the war was not a great surprise. As I had been required to guard the school on a regular basis (every third or fourth night) against South Korean intruders and vandalism, I had listened to the troops and tank movements while on duty. The sounds of tanks and armored vehicles passing on the street approximately two hundred yards away from school during the curfew hours had been almost constant since the end of May. It seemed that the armored vehicles were most likely going to the 38th parallel. I had anticipated that the war would begin shortly but had no idea that it would happen just when it did. My duties in watching the school were in addition to my regular teaching schedule, which was only modified to permit me to skip my first class (so I could catch a little additional sleep after my night duties) with a substitute teacher taking over my first class. Prior to the sounds of rumbling tanks, there had been peace talks between the delegates of North and South Korea for a possible reunification of the divided country, but the peace talks failed due to the disagreement over which side would play the dominant role in the new government. Of course the country did not want to be divided, and the North Koreans pressured the South Koreans to unify with North Korea under North Korean auspices. However, the government of Syngman Rhee was not prepared to allow the Communist North to take over and refused to continue the talks along those lines. On June 19, 1950, a "Supreme People's Assembly" had been convened of left-leaning South Koreans, as well as North Korean delegates. The assembly met in Pyongyang to call for "free elections" that were intended to result in a favorable result for North Korea and would unify the country under the hegemony of the North Korean-Soviet axis.[2]

The sounds of the army heading in the direction of the 38th parallel made me recognize that the North Korean government had been preparing for attack all along. Although the populace recognized that war was shortly to be upon them, they did not openly discuss the matter. The atmosphere in North Korea was very tense; no one could speak freely about the upcoming war. There were spies from the Communist Party in every corner of Korean society; they would not hesitate to send naysayers to Siberia in punishment.

Kim Il-Sung had been sending guerrilla units into the South since March. The orders of the spies were to disrupt transport and communications after the war had begun. Although initially provided with food and weapons, the spies were directed to steal whatever they required from dead or captured enemy troops. Although the South Koreans had been realistic enough to order certain major bridges to be wired for explosives, it quickly became evident that the North Koreans had disabled the explosive charges, permitting the North Koreans to swarm unhindered toward the South. Additionally many of the

South Korean army units that were supposed to be defending Seoul were de-pleted, as many of the soldiers were on weekend leave.[3]

The North Koreans conquered Seoul very quickly (within a few days) with little resistance from South Korean troops and soon developed a reputation for ferocity. The North Koreans quickly executed members of the South Korean cabinet, as well as members of the police force who had played a leading role in anti-communism or were formerly pro-Japanese. However, the rape of South Korean women was severely punished. In August 1950, I was informally invited to a court-martial in the city of Pyongyang by my close friend, Master Sergeant Ko of the North Korean Army. He was in charge of the guards within the city water district. At the trial, I saw one North Korean soldier who had raped a South Korean woman in Seoul demoted in rank, humiliated, and sentenced to a hard-labor camp in Siberia after having given a public apology to all those in attendance at the trial. Self-evaluation was part of the punishment for nearly every crime.

After the establishment of the North Korean government in 1947, the So-viets had begun to withdraw their troops from North Korea except for their military/political advisors and its technicians. Likewise the American troops and its civilian workers had also withdrawn from South Korea.

Ever since the Russian invasion, Russia's "military advisors" and key per-sonnel had trained North Korean troops around the clock with the end view that the North Koreans would invade South Korea and remove an obstacle to Russian hegemony in the region. The North Korean government established a curfew of 10 P.M. about two to three months before the Korean War started, probably to ensure that there were as few people on the streets as possible to witness their war preparations. In keeping with the perceived expectations of their Russian masters, the North Koreans obligingly attacked South Korea on June 25, 1950. Immediately after the war started, the South Korean president, Syngman Rhee, presented the issue of North Korean aggression at the United Nations. The U.N. then voted unanimously to send police forces from various countries, including the U.S. and Great Britain, to Korea to defend South Korea. Except for the U.S. air bombing in Korea, U.S. combat troops did not come to South Korea until about the first part of September in 1950. By then the North Korean troops occupied almost the entire region of South Korea with the exception of the vicinity of Pusan, which is the southernmost city of Korea and had a strategic naval base.

According to a South Korean friend whom I eventually met later in South Korea at the 1ˢᵗ FOB and to whom I became attached as a support worker, part of the reason that the North Koreans defeated the South Koreans so quickly was that some North Korean secret agents had inserted themselves into the South Korean army, attained a high rank within the South Korean army, and were then in a position to persuade a South Korean general to send a quantity of soldiers home on furlough without their weapons with the excuse that rations could be saved and the excess rations be sold on the black market for money. The money could then be deposited in the general's personal account. Also the soldiers were largely draftees from small farming communities, and they were persuaded to help their families working in the field while they were on leave on weekend. Consequently it was quite advantageous from the North Korean strategic point of view to advance deep inside South Korea rapidly as there was so little resistance from the South Korean army.

The first few months of U.S. air bombing in North Korea after the South was attacked was limited to military targets and usually occurred on Sunday mornings. Afterwards the bombings became indiscriminate without any predictable schedule. Many civilians lost their homes and lives. The two major reasons that the American Air Force bombed civilian targets were as follows: (1) to instill panic and create an uprising against the North Korean government; (2) many North Koreans used civilian facilities as protection against bombing, e.g., churches and schools. American leaflets warning against bombing were destroyed by police before they could be read by the populace. Civilians were not allowed to pick up the leaflets, which could only be picked up by the police.

However, a local police sergeant who picked up the leaflets and was a good friend occasionally allowed me to read them. (This was the same person who had earlier taken me to the North Korean military court and allowed me to watch the trial of a North Korean army officer who had raped a South Korean woman.)

The first U.S. bomber that I spotted was a U.S. Navy jet, which seemed to be an odd sort of plane in that it did not have a propeller. I prayed for the U.S. pilot's safety, hoping that he would be in the front of a rescue mission that would save North Korea from the terrible government that had been imposed upon us. When word came that the U.S. pilot had crashed near a farm village of Presbyterian Christians near where my stepmother had come from, a family in the village saved the pilot in their attic, providing the pilot with food and clothes. When the U.S. invaded Pyongyang in December 1950, the Koreans handed the U.S. pilot back. However, when the Communists regained control, the Communists burned the house where the pilot had been sequestered, killing the entire family.

U.S. bombing destroyed most of the bridges crossing the Tadong River. Those bridges that were not destroyed completely were left tilted at an angle, rendering them useless for streetcars and difficult to walk for foot traffic. Civilians immediately went to work repairing the bridges, mostly at night to avoid American bombing. The narrowing of the river that I had participated in as a civilian volunteer was done to permit the North Korean Army to move their tanks over the wooden bridge that the civilian volunteers had created.

Civilians were not allowed to leave Pyongyang unless they were aged or infirm. Although I saw the dreadful results of the Pyongyang bombings during my travels back and forth between the city water compound and the elementary school where I taught, American bombing did not occur near the city water compound area until September 1950. One morning I went outside after a bombing raid and saw blown-off legs dangling from the power lines. Shortly thereafter Grandfather died after a bombing raid (he was seventy-four at the time) when a glass window shattered over his body, cutting his face severely. He had been sick for about two months, and one day when the bombing occurred, the window shattered over his face, killing him immediately. This was very hard on Grandmother, who had loved her husband very much.

Although the North Korean military had projected an image of relentless toughness at the beginning of the Korean War, the army was composed mainly of poor farming boys drafted by the government. Although most of them had no quarrel with the U.S., once in the Army, they were compelled to advance against U.S. lines by the Communist soldiers at the rear of each unit. There was no possibility of retreat or surrender, as the Communists were given strict orders to shoot soldiers who failed to perform their duty.

One soldier I remembered specifically for his less-than-full commitment to the North Korean side of the war was the master sergeant who was in charge of the North Korean guard at the city water compound where I lived. I had become friendly with the master sergeant to the extent that once, when the American bombers dropped leaflets warning of an impending attack, I was able to pick up a leaflet and stuff it into my pocket in full view of the master sergeant, who pretended not to notice. Ordinary Koreans who picked up such leaflets were usually denounced immediately to the government.

It was painful, therefore, to see the master sergeant suffer and die during the advance of the South Korean and American forces into Pyongyang. A one point, the master sergeant had been so severely wounded that he had taken refuge in a sewer pipe. The next day he was unceremoniously routed from his safe haven. The South Korean army lieutenant who had discovered him dispatched him with three shots of his pistol, lingering between each discharge of the gun to increase the suffering of the master sergeant. The South Korean lieutenant made no attempt to hide his actions from me (I happened to be standing nearby) and ordered me to go home after the master sergeant finally died. I was able to retrieve the master sergeant's billfold, which contained a picture of the man's wife and children, but was ordered to go home and leave the master sergeant's body by the side of the road. The next day an American soldier appeared at the door of my home and ordered all the male occupants of the house to help bury the bodies left from the previous day's fighting. While others gathered the remaining soldiers into a large mound stacked like firewood and eventually buried them in a mass grave without benefit of ceremony or coffins, I dragged the body of the master sergeant a little way away from the others into a wooded area, where I buried the master sergeant with as much feeling and solemnity as I could muster.

My friend, Sgt. Ko, had allowed me to attend the rapist's trial, inasmuch as it would allow the North Korean Army to display its ethical nature and conduct to the world. The fact that it would publicly condemn and humiliate the criminals within its midst would be an example of the North Korean government's honesty, forthrightness, and adherence to universal principles of morality and justice. The master sergeant hoped that I would be a useful propaganda tool as a teacher in the government's efforts to win the hearts and minds of the populace and obtain credibility with the outside world.

The trial of the rapist involved having the man perform all the actions in mime that he had done on the hapless South Korean victim.

I was also allowed to visit an American POW camp, where I was exposed to the North Korean philosophy of ideology propagation. The master sergeant took me through the camp and showed me the prisoner environs. Essentially there were two POW areas of the camp. The first area, for the recalcitrant soldiers who resisted indoctrination, required the prisoners to labor hard in the prison garden, raising food and performing other types of hard labor as required. Despite their heavy chores, the first group of prisoners was still required to attend classes in Marxism and the Soviet system. Those who proved themselves to be adaptable and disposed to learn the subject matter would be allowed to eventually join the second group of prisoners. The second group was composed of POWs who were more disposed to listen to their captor's dissertations and were amenable to their purposes. The second group would often be at liberty while the first group was hard at work, usually playing volleyball with the North Korean guards at noontime and listening attentively in the indoctrination classes. The master sergeant emphasized that the North Korean government did not hate the American people, only the U.S. government. The master sergeant told me that he hoped that the POWs when released would return to America and spread the Marxist doctrine, fomenting revolution to destroy the existing government and its leaders.

Despite the master sergeant's bland assurances regarding the superiority of communism, it is significant that after the end of the Korean war, twenty-five thousand North Korean POWs applied to remain in South Korea.[4]

Another thing that the master sergeant related was that North Koreans in battle would try to be captured by the Americans, if possible, instead of the South Koreans. South Koreans, on the other hand, would try to be captured by the Chinese instead of the North Koreans.

While visiting the camp, I was invited to play a game of volleyball with the American POWs. Reluctantly I did so with the mater sergeant's assurances that each participation would foster goodwill with the Americans.

"After all," said the master sergeant, "why should we hate Americans? The Americans and our great Soviet Russian Army together delivered us from the Japanese. And I'm sure the Japanese taught you the Confucian principle of loving your enemies. 'If a man hits you on one cheek, turn to him the other.'"

I responded rather indignantly. "I believe that your reference to Confucius may not be appropriate. According to party teachings, religion is anti-revolutionary."

The master sergeant responded, "You must realize that Confucianism is a philosophy, not a religion. If you were brought up in this society, whether you were brought up as Buddhist, Christian, or Hindu, the prevailing philosophy was Confucian. Do not make the mistake of confusing philosophy with religion."

So with certain misgivings about what my superiors might think if they ever heard of it, I stepped up to the volleyball net.

"Hey, shorty, let's see what you can do!" came the joking remark from one of the GIs.

This rankled me to the point where I responded, "My name is not Shorty" in rather broken English. I proceeded to deliver a serve with such spin on it that the ball bounded off the tips of the American serviceman's fingers and went out of bounds. It gave me a sense of satisfaction in being able to show what a short person could do!

On the other hand, I saw that the North Koreans caught some GIs and forced them to walk barefoot toward Pyongyang on black asphalt under the hot sun. They had people watch as they walked toward the prisoner compound, and when the spectators attempted to throw stones, they were beaten back by the North Korean guards. This was quite different from the American POWs playing volleyball with North Korean guards in their POW camp. Although there were some POWs who were at hard labor trying to grow crops in their compound, these troops were also learning about communism. North Korea hoped to send these unwilling captives also back to America where they would spread the communist message.

Civilians, especially women and children, are victims of war — any war. In the midst of the summer of 1951 during the Korean War, I went to my public school playground to see if any of the classes were being held. Suddenly the city's warning siren was turned on loud to make everyone aware of the fact that there was an air raid by about fifty American B-17 bombers. I crossed under the foxhole that had been dug by the students in the early part of the month. The foxhole was about a foot and a half wide and six feet deep from the surface of the playground. The roof of the foxhole was made of a few tree branch logs and sheet metal and covered with about ten inches of dirt. Among the other classmates (about twenty of them), I crawled inside the foxhole and waited for the air raid to be over. Within fifteen minutes, I felt the entire foxhole walls vibrate, and dirt fell over my head and shoulders. By then I knew that we were hit by bombs off the bombers. Many teachers and other college students were afraid of staying inside the foxhole and attempted to run away from the foxhole. Unfortunately they were hit by the fragments of bombs before they even ran fifty yards from the foxhole. I remained within the foxhole and put my head down, covering it with my hands and arms. After about thirty minutes or so, things began to quiet down. I then cautiously crawled out of the foxhole and saw many dead bodies lying on the ground. An infant child was crying over her mother's dead body. Those who ran to the hills also died by the hundreds when the bombers came back to bomb both the school compound and the hillside.

I did not see any trace of bombed holes on the ground, except for a few small holes around six inches deep and ten inches in diameter. Later I learned that it was the first time in the Korean War that Americans experimented with the small bombs that can explode sideways (within a ten-foot range) as soon as they hit the ground. I saw at least 230 such holes over the school playground. The object of using such bombs was to kill ground troops without damaging structures. Instead of killing ground troops, this air raid created civilian casualties by the hundreds. At this point, I did not care who won the war, except that it should end as quickly as possible. Exiting my foxhole, I finally made it home after about three hours of having to pass over bridges that were nearly destroyed and avoiding the numerous fires and other destruction that reigned in the wake of the bombing. My father was not there when I got home; he finally came in the next morning, as he spent the entire night trying to assist the wounded.

During this time, my father was asked to join the Communist Party. My father hated the Communists, having lost all his land to the Communists and seeing what a shambles the Communists had made of the government and the political infrastructure. However, not wanting to have an active confrontation over the matter, he kept postponing such a commitment, preferring to point out that he was not certain that he would be a good prospective member, having been a white-collar worker under the Japanese and having benefited from their rule. Although we never spoke directly of it, I knew he hoped that I would go to America and leave the wreck of the country that North Korea had become. His steadfast reluctance gained the enmity of the party, and eventually the party sent two workers to learn my father's job.

With the intense U.S. bombing, our food supplies dwindled markedly. There was little being transported to market, and with the highly inflated currency, we could buy little of it. Our family still had little to eat and was reduced to eating only one meal per day, mostly from what we could raise in our garden — vegetables which were largely converted into kimchi. We had managed to raise one pig in a five-foot by five-foot by six-foot bunker, which we finally had to sell; it was dragged away kicking and screaming. Unfortunately we could not preserve enough of it for a long enough period of time to keep us all fed. I very much regretted having to sell the pig, as it had almost become a pet.

The U.S. bombing became so intense that the North Korean government finally allowed the women and children to exit Pyongyang. All our relatives decided to go their separate ways. My aunt had decided to try to get to the family farm (near Pyongyang) and stay there, at least until the American troops had come over. My maternal grandmother went to live with her nephew in a small fishing village about twenty-five miles away from Pyongyang. Gen. MacArthur finally landed at Inchon Harbor next to the city of Pyongyang. The harbor was bombed for four days prior to the U.S. Marines's landing. Once having landed, the marines headed north, planning to conquer the North Korean troops all the way to the Yalu River. However, this objective was frustrated, in that MacArthur's forces were stopped at Hamung by the Chinese troops. The winter was bitterly cold, and the U.S. troops were ill-prepared for the cold. By the time the U.S. troops made it to Hamung, they had been surrounded by the North Koreans and Chinese for about one month. Many died in battle or experienced severe frostbite prior to evacuation by U.S. Navy.

Upon the landing of U.S. forces in North Korea, all able-bodied young men were immediately subject to the draft. I was not a candidate for the draft being a teacher, but Youngchan, who was attending an agricultural college, was eligible. Although we sequestered Youngchan in the attic of the house to prevent him from being kidnapped off the streets by the roving North Korean Army (who were at that time looking for enlistees), at last a pink slip came to inform Youngchan that he needed to report to the draft office. The night prior to Youngchan's appointment with the draft office, my father got very little sleep due to worry over Youngchan's fate.

Before Youngchan left for the draft office, I created a message that said "I don't want to fight, I am being forced to fight" and put it in a sack attached to Youngchan's neck. In the event that he was immediately drafted into the North Korean Army and ultimately captured by the Americans, I hoped that this message might prove to be Youngchan's salvation. However, the doctor who was in charge of the exam flunked Youngchan on the basis of flat feet. We were greatly relieved that there was no need for Youngchan to hide in the attic thereafter!

Fortunately we had sort of a makeshift bunker during the time of the bombings, which was really a tunnel used to house pipes as they passed from the city water island to the city water area where we lived. We perceived it as safe (it being constructed of thick concrete) and allowed it to be used only by the family and city water department workers.

Upon hearing of the advance of the U.S. troops and South Korean troops into Pyongyang well in advance, it gave our family an opportunity to hide in the transfer tunnel, which indeed proved to be safe although many of the North Korean troops were killed in nearby cement pipelines. Although there were South Korean troops lodged in the compound below the city water area where the Japanese troops had been formerly stationed, judging by the flags on top of the compound, no South Korean troops ever made it into the premises of the city water compound itself where we lived. The house in the city water compound was badly damaged with many bullet holes on the interior and exterior. The house's supporting columns were severely damaged, and all the windows and all the mirrors had been broken.

The South Korean troops took full advantage of the opportunity to discharge their wrath on the North Korean inhabitants. I had seen my friend, the North Korean policeman who had allowed me to read the American leaflets and who had taken me to see the trial of the North Korean officer charged with rape of a South Korean woman, terribly beaten by the South Koreans. Eventually they wound up shooting him in the head five times before he stopped asking for help. The South Korean officer who opened his wallet found a picture of his wife and child and discovered he was a draftee from a poor farming family. Although I retrieved the wallet, I had no way of returning the wallet to the man's family.

A few days later, the U.S. troops arrived. As they had arrived somewhat later and appeared to be fairly fresh-looking, I doubted they were engaged in the battle. Many of the U.S. military police came by to make sure the water was not contaminated. Fortunately the water was still clean, but the U.S. soldiers refused to drink it, importing their water instead from Hawaii.

Upon arrival at the compound, the U.S. soldiers made the family and the workers retrieve the bodies of the North Korean soldiers and put them into a mass grave near the house. By this time, the bodies had begun to decompose and were creating a horrible smell. I felt very badly for the North Koreans who had been forced to fight against their will, leaving their families to fend for themselves in the surrounding farming communities. The Americans now occupied the compound, though the South Koreans were kept nearby, doing target practice. During one such target practice, a bullet flew by my ear, signaling a need for caution when venturing out-of-doors.

The Americans were somewhat of a revelation to the Rhee family. There were seven of them. They brought their own rations (unlike the Russians, who had stolen what they required from the populace) and shared their tinned corned beef with our family. Although we were not surprised by the presence of red-haired, blue-eyed people, having been acquainted with the U.S. missionaries, the presence of a black soldier in the compound was a real surprise. The black soldier, Harmon, was from Washington, D.C. Having understood from the Communist propaganda that black people had been reduced to slavery in the U.S., I frankly asked him why a black soldier was fighting with American troops. When he informed me that he was a citizen of the U.S., I was quite frankly surprised. Upon the arrival of the U.S. troops, Father took the opportunity to discharge the Communist employee who was supposed to take over his job. I am certain that this action would have provided the final "nail in the coffin" for my father, who would certainly have been executed after the withdrawal of the American troops from North Korea.

Slowly our family made contact with one another again. When my grandmother had discovered that my aunt, who had moved back to her farming community, had been raped by six American soldiers with little resistance, she became very angry. The soldiers had been kind to her niece's daughter, giving the daughter candy, and were able to take advantage of my aunt's naiveté.

Unfortunately the presence of the Americans and the South Koreans did not win the hearts and minds of all of the North Koreans. I met a friend who expressed his hatred for the South Korean troops who raped their women, robbed their country, and who began creating another round of inflation.

Despite the advent of war and the invasion of North Korea by the Americans and the South Koreans, I had the good fortune to encounter representatives of the 171st Field Army Hospital when they first entered Pyongyang looking to find a base of operations. The forward observers of the first FOB were the heart and soul of the unit. They only numbered about twenty men out of three hundred men in the unit, but the rest of the soldiers worked in support of them, either directly or indirectly The forward observers were charged with identifying enemy-troop movements in the field and for calling artillery strikes in on selected targets. Their function as frontline spies meant their lives were in constant danger on the battlefield, especially as they carried only carbines and pistols, not M-1 rifles. They definitely had the most difficult and dangerous duty judging by the condition of their clothes upon returning from a mission. The time frame when I initially encountered the Americans was during the first week of November 1950, about a month after Chusok and a month after the South Korean and American troops came to Pyongyang and pushed the North Korean troops back almost up to Yalu River. Although Pyongyang was being occupied by South Korean troops, mostly a ROK (Republic of Korea) Army police force, no provisional government had been set up.

Although I was not teaching school during that time because of the intensive fighting going on in Pyongyang, I wanted to see the condition of Pyongyang Normal School, where I had previously taught second and third grades for two years. There were no streetcars running in Pyongyang due to the bombing from the air, as well as the fighting on the ground. As the school was about four miles from my house and located on the other side of the Tadong River, Youngchan, Han Rokun (an employee of the city water department and my father's close friend), and I made the journey together for safety's sake. The bridge, which was three miles from my house, was partially destroyed and inclined at about a fifteen-degree angle from the horizontal. Walking across the bridge was a bit nerve-wracking due not only to its inclination, but doubts about its structural stability. From the end of the bridge, it was about another mile's walk to the school.

Although I had hoped that the school would be able to be fixed up so that I could resume my teaching, I discovered that about one-quarter of the elementary school buildings were demolished and would have to be repaired before classes could resume. The likelihood that my career was on indefinite hold was heartbreaking; not only did I enjoy teaching the children, but I also taught other novice student teachers who were in their last year of teacher's college. Pyongyang Normal School was directly associated with the teacher's college, and only the outstanding teachers were allowed to teach at this elementary school. The damaged school and the ongoing battles seemed to spell an end to my future hopes and plans.

After leaving the school playground, I determined to enroll in the South Korean Air Force, as did Han Rokun, who had also at one time worked for the Japanese Air Force. Although we stopped by a South Korean Air Force post on our way back home and tried to persuade the local South Korean guard to permit us to enter and enlist, the guard did not permit us to enter the post.

On our way back home, I was stopped by three American trucks in front of the city hall that were recruiting Korean labor. The truck took us to the 171st Army Hospital, which was then located in one of Pyongyang's major civilian hospitals and which had originally been built by the Japanese. There were about 150 Koreans who had been transported in the truck by the American MPs lined up on the hospital grounds being scrutinized as potential laborers. When asked whether any of the assembled group could speak English, I tentatively raised my hand. I stepped forward as one who could speak English at the urging of one of the South Korean interpreters who spoke with me briefly. My limited knowledge of English, obtained from my studies at teacher's college, got me a job as a houseboy with Dr. Tetreault and Dr. Marshall B. Atkinson, both surgeons at the 171st Field Army hospital, really a MASH unit. My brother Youngchan, who previously attended agricultural college in Pyongyang, was assigned to mop the floors in the hospital emergency rooms and other areas, such as bathrooms, until another job could be opened up for him. That evening Youngchan and I were prevented from leaving due to the fact that the ROK Army had set up curfew hours for civilians at night. I was also not able to phone home to let my father know what had happened. Although I was informed that I could sleep in Dr. Tetreault's office, Youngchan was assigned to sleep in the officers' bathroom, so I slept there as well, not wanting him to feel as if I had abandoned him. The next day I went to Dr. Tetreault's office, where the doctor quizzed me about Korean customs and history. He informed me that I would be responsible for cleaning the surgical rooms, the bathrooms, and taking care of his personal clothing, as well as for providing any needed translation services, but that I would not be responsible for any heavy labor. These duties usually only required two to three hours per day.

With encouragement from Dr. Tetreault, I fortunately was able to spend more time learning English so as to be more useful to them.

One afternoon Dr. Tetreault gave me money for doughnuts, but not knowing what doughnuts were, I bought cookies instead. The money I was given was red dollar bills printed for U.S. armed forces (called GI currency in the war zone) and was unusable outside the war zone.

I worked at the hospital for about four to five weeks prior to the Chinese and North Korean counterattack when the U.S. and South Korean forces were edging up toward the Yalu River. I was greatly concerned for my family's well-being and also held forth the hope that I could one day go back to teaching in my Pyongyang school. I could not face the idea of leaving my family behind, so I decided to discontinue working for the hospital. I explained the situation as best I could to Dr. Tetreault, feeling very guilty about it all the while, as I knew that my translation services sometimes were in great demand. Nevertheless, Dr. Tetreault took it in good part and told me, "I understand your situation, and you have to do what is the best for your future…." He gave me a good letter of recommendation, assuring me that he would be more than willing to help in the future if need be. A week after quitting work at the U.S. Army hospital, the Chinese were advancing rapidly from Yalu River (located at borderline of Manchuria and Korea) toward Pyongyang (almost twenty-five miles each day), and the artillery sound kept getting closer and louder each night. Simultaneously the U.S. and South Korean troops appeared to be evacuating south as the Chinese kept pouring over the border.

I soon regretted quitting the hospital so soon and briefly debated trying to go back to the field hospital with the hope that I might be able to evacuate to south with the 171st Hospital, but I felt as if I had no face to try to go back there.

Returning home I discovered that the family was still there, although the situation was as bad as when I had left the home previously about a month earlier. The Chinese were pushing forward down from the Yalu River and attacking the U.S. and South Koreans ferociously, although they were, by all accounts, underequipped for battle. According to rumor, only one in three soldiers had a rifle. Nevertheless, their guerrilla tactics were such as to create an impression of a much larger, well-fortified force, and in tandem with the North

Korean army, the tide of battle was soon turned against the Americans and South Koreans. Although the Americans and South Koreans had taken over approximately two-thirds of North Korea, they began retreating steadily.

About a week after Youngchan, Han Rokun, and I had returned to our home in the city water compound area, at 3 A.M. the cannons and other artillery began to shoot in earnest. We could hear the sounds of battle moving ever closer and deemed it likely that it would only be a matter of hours until our home was directly in the middle of the battle zone.

My father decided to send Heechan, along with all the family pictures, to her aunt's home approximately two miles away, deeming that she might be safer there. Although I never saw or heard from Heechan again, I later learned that there were South Korean troops in the area over which she was traveling, and I can only say that I fear she may have not have made it to safety.

My father strongly encouraged both Youngchan and I to leave home and head south, as he knew that there was little chance of anyone surviving who remained in that situation. Also there was every likelihood that Youngchan and I would be forced to serve in the North Korean Army if we remained, a prospect that I could not possibly entertain. Although my grandmother implored Youngchan and I to stay with the family, there was no possibility of taking her, my father, or Inchan, my youngest brother, south with us, as the hardships of travel would be too great, and there would be no possibility for us to look after them in the event that they actually were able to make it to the south. Also I still hoped beyond hope that the war would end soon and that we could rejoin our family in North Korea under the auspices of a more reasonable and tolerant government installed by the Americans and the South Koreans.

As we initially thought, it would have been far too dangerous and difficult for our family to have gone with us to South Korea. Not only was the actual journey to South Korea extremely difficult for us (three able-bodied men), but after arriving in South Korea, there would have been little we could have done to help our family members even though we were able to make contact with the American troops. South Korea at that time was in the midst of an extremely difficult time, during which many experienced extraordinary hardship and loss. Our family's fate in the hands of the South Koreans could well have been worse than would have been the case by remaining in North Korea.

Endnotes

1. Max Hastings, *The Korean War* (New York: Simon & Schuster, 1987), 323, 329.
2. Stanley Weintraub, *MacArthur's War: Korea and the Undoing of an American Hero* (New York: Free Press, 2000), 8, 22, 28-29.
3. See note 2 above.
4. See note 1 above.

Chapter VIII
Huck and Youngchan Go South

*A*t my father's urging, Youngchan and I finally decided to leave Pyongyang sometime during the first part of December 1950. The Chinese troops were closing in fast, the American forces (who had at one time occupied nearly two-thirds of North Korea) were in retreat, and I did not wish to be caught by the Chinese or North Korean troops and pressed into service, especially after having served with the American troops for a month. One night Youngchan, Han Rokun (a city water employee who had been a personal friend of my father's), and I decided to leave quietly in the middle of the night. Although Grandmother had requested us to stay, I felt that I could not do so. Our sister, Heechan, had fled to our aunt's house with all the family pictures, and we had not heard anything from her for several hours. I hoped that Youngchan and I would only be away for a short time until the Americans were able to return, but I feared the worst. I told my father that I hoped to be back in about two weeks after the Americans had returned.

Despite concern for our family, we decided to head south in the direction of the retreating American troops. We went looking for a bridge to cross the Ta Dong River, which divides the northern and southern parts of Pyongyang, but all of them had been completely obliterated. We finally found a small boat, which took us part way across the river, but the river itself was partially frozen. We wound up having to walk on the frozen surface of the river to the other side.

Having made it across the river, we immediately went to the house of Father's close friend, Uncle Sok, where we stayed that evening. He provided warm clothes, food, and a bed for the night. Uncle Sok's daughter had gone off to South Korea with the South Korean Army thinking that she would be able to obtain protection and employment in South Korea. However, according to the source of information, all the girls who went off with the South Korean army had been raped by their officers. We went to bed early, but by 2:30 A.M., an artillery shell landed fifty yards away from Uncle Sok's house. We finally had to leave his house due to the artillery shells that were landing so close. The Americans had begun their intense bombing campaign of Pyongyang. After leaving Uncle Sok's house, Youngchan, Han Rokun, and I walked seven miles till we had entered the countryside; by then it was dawn. We came to a Korean farmer's house, where we heard the cow lowing at us. Knocking on the door, we told the farmer about the intense bombing and that we were trying to travel south. He invited us in for breakfast before allowing us to continue our journey. After breakfast we continued traveling along the same road. Although it was an agricultural area, there were houses every two hundred to three hundred yards. I was pleased that Han Rokun, who had been working for the city water institution under my father, also came down with Youngchan and me. Han Rokun was a year younger than I and sometimes drank socially with my father. He was unmarried and had only his mother to look after. He was a very humorous fellow and very kind to his mother, as well as to my family. He had a dark complexion and lived in the city water compound next to our family's residence. After breakfast and having walked for two hours, we ran into a South Korean military police checkpoint. We told the MP that we were refugees from North Korea, that we wanted to go south. The MPs told us that the South Korean Army would shortly be in Pyongyang and that it was unnecessary for us to go south. The MPs said that the South Koreans would conquer North Korea in a matter of weeks. Unfortunately Han Rokun disputed this assertion directly (i.e., that the South Korean troops would conquer Pyongyang) and received a severe beating from the South Korean MPs. Fortunately I was not beaten — probably because I did not confront them, as well as my status as a teacher. Youngchan was also too young and mild-mannered to be beaten. Retreating from the hostile response that we had received from the South Korean MPs, we managed to walk away and circle back through the mountains during the day. We met another traveler on the trail, also a former native of North Korea, who tried to persuade us to return to North Korea, saying that the situation in South Korea was very bad in that there was lots of corruption, violence, and raping of women. However, we chose to disregard the advice, thinking that perhaps the man was a North Korean agent. We eventually fell in with another group of refugees traveling south who wore white clothes to make it clear that they were civilians.

By late in the evening, we approached a small farm town on the outskirts of Pyongyang that was demolished, except for the train station and the railways. There was a train there with an open bed full of American artillery but with no cover on the train. It was fortunate for us that the American train cars had the same size rail gauge as the Korean cars, unlike the rails in Japan, whose cars had a different gauge. The train was operated by American soldiers in concert with Korean employees. They agreed to take the three of us, along with many other North Korean refugees, to the south. The train had a wooden floor, but as it was uncovered, it was quite cold. The three of us had only one blanket between us. It began snowing as well. The following day at about 7 A.M., the train stopped, and the three of us had to walk from there on. The train had traveled for a day and night and dropped the three of us, as well as the other civilian refugees, inside South Korea, about twenty-five miles from the 38th parallel line. We were in the open with no village around. We had to walk on railroad ties on the track that extended over what I believe, in retrospect, to have been a small tributary of the Han River near what I believe to be the current Panmunjan outpost. At one time, we had to hang onto the narrow side platforms along the ties as the train passed. By the time we had walked nearly seven miles, the soles of our shoes started to form large holes and cause much discomfort to our feet. Walking became difficult and painful. Fortunately a farmer with a carriage passed by and offered to take us to the outskirts of Seoul in his carriage for free.

We stayed in a motel on the first night in South Korea on the outskirts of Seoul, having arrived there at about 11 P.M. To stay in that motel overnight, we paid the equivalent of two weeks of my teacher's salary in North Korea due to South Korean inflation. The room itself was cold and dark, and although we requested heat for the room, the motel owner only put one candle in the "ondal" (a fire bed under the floor). The following morning, without having had any breakfast, we went looking for the 171st Field Army Hospital where I used to work in Pyongyang for Dr. Tetreault and Dr. Atkinson. We looked until 8 P.M. We crossed the Han River on foot in the cold and dark and reached an American checkpoint at the town of Yong-don-po. Although we had arrived at the 171st Field Army Hospital, Dr. Tetreault was not there at the time. However, we met Dr. Atkinson, who greeted us and gave us each a can of tuna fish, corned beef and crackers, and field jackets to wear. After not having anything to eat for last couple days, the canned food was very tasty. The 171st Hospital was loading its gear in preparation for going to Japan, with Dr. Atkinson being ordered to go with them. Dr. Atkinson explained that while they were evacuating from Pyongyang, Dr. Tetreault had transferred to the 1st Artillery Army Field Observation Battalion. Dr. Atkinson mentioned that Dr. Tetreault was due to pick up medical supplies at almost any time. Within twenty minutes after the three of us had arrived at the 171st, Dr. Tetreault finally arrived. I related the story of our harrowing trip down to South Korea. Dr. Tetreault took us to the 1st Field Artillery Observation Battalion in his Jeep. I asked Dr. Tetreault whether I could have my old position as houseboy with him. Dr. Tetreault indicated that he could use me but not Youngchan or Han Rokun. I settled down in Dr. Tetreault's tent and prayed to my deceased mother for help. I could not bear separating from the last member of my family, knowing that both Youngchan and Han Rokun would likely be forced to fight in the frontlines against the North Korean troops, but I saw no other course. However, the next day the mess sergeant indicated that he was able to hire Youngchan and Han Rokun on KP duty. I believe my deceased mother heard my prayer and was able to respond.

Life with the 1st FOB was a sanctuary compared to the time spent in North Korea. During the time in 1st FOB, I experienced great concern for my family, not knowing whether my family had been killed. I was especially concerned that my family, especially my father, had been killed by the Communists. I often had nightmares about my family, sometimes waking up in the middle of the night. The amount of time I spent in South Korea was from December 1950 through March 1954.

The duties with 1st FOB were to work with GIs in different departments. 1st FOB had a headquarters battery, as well as A, B, and C batteries, scattered thirty to fifty miles apart. The overall function of the 1st FOB was to observe enemy movements, calculate their position using topographical maps, and direct fire (signal to the artillery division) toward the areas where the scouts had indicated. Scouts, being American, would be killed immediately if the enemy discovered them. Both Youngchan and I worked for the HQ FOB. My duties were to be both a houseboy and a translator for the doctors and work for the medical detachment doing normal household chores, such as packing and unpacking, making beds, preparing shaving kits, etc. The 1st FOB moved back and forth depending on the location of Chinese troops. The 1st FOB moved seventy to one hundred miles with respect to the 38th parallel line at least fifty times. We all lived in tents, and each one of us had to help build sandbag fortifications in order to help protect the living quarters of the doctors. Our medical detachment personnel were generally well-educated and mostly college graduates. The individual doctors tended to be very friendly and not rough and profane, as was the case of other U.S. soldiers we sometimes encountered.

Both Youngchan and I were provided with clothes and food, as well as carbines, and paid twenty-five dollars per month. Youngchan and Han Rokun were assigned to the mess hall working for the field kitchen mess sergeant. The KP duties were much rougher than what I had to deal with in my life, inasmuch as Youngchan and Han Rokun had to get up at 4 A.M., pump fourteen gas stoves for lighting, and help with food service to the GIs. Afterward they had to clean up the pots, pans, and dishes — all in the freezing cold during the dead of winter — with chapped hands. They did this for three meals every day. Additionally the two of them had to help the mess hall move locations approximately every two months depending on the battle situation. GIs who worked in the mess hall were rough. They tended to give tongue-lashings to Korean employees. Sometimes the mess sergeant would shoot at the Korean refugees (mostly women with children) to keep them from taking food from the garbage cans. Despite this, Youngchan got along very well with the GIs, who called him Di-Di.

During the winter of 1951, the 1st FOB was experiencing the full fury of battle for the first time. The 1st FOB was not a combat battalion, so it was ill-prepared for the battle stresses it was forced to experience. As the 1st FOB kept pushing into North Korea, it became, by default, the shock troops for the various combat divisions that were following it. China was entering its first battle with the U.S.; as the U.S. started pushing the North Korean troops out of

South Korea, the Chinese realized that they needed to resist the U.S. The Chinese were not well-equipped with weapons — only one rifle purchased from the U.K. per two or three soldiers — though they did have mortars. Mostly they had lots of soldiers. They pressed past the city of Tagoo, causing the U.S. and U. N. troops to retreat southward. 1st FOB and the 3rd Army Artillery Division were assigned to block off the Chinese. They headed north to meet the Chinese and head them off. One of my first major duties with the 1st FOB was to pack gear for doctors when they moved near the Imjin River near the 38th parallel in January 1951. We drove north into an old wheat field that was partially harvested, covered with snow, and about fifty yards away from a main highway. The ground was heavily furrowed and frozen, with daytime temperatures averaging about eight degrees Fahrenheit and nighttime temperatures averaging about minus-twenty degrees. The frozen, furrowed ground made for lumps under the tent floors in the doctor's tents despite the fact that bulldozers flattened the ground for major portions of the encampment. Most soldiers were left to erect their own tents as best they could despite the presence of the furrowed ground. In large measure, the site was chosen due to its location near the 3rd Army Artillery Division and the ability to hide in the furrows in the event of a wide-scale attack. A temporary bridge was built across the river using rope and floating rubber boats. The first night after arrival, Youngchan and I were assigned to stand guard at different posts, with two hours of guard duty and two hours of sleep time. The guard post was about seven feet in diameter, with two feet worth of sandbags all around. A machine-gun post was set up in the middle of the post. Fortunately there were heavy clothes available (field jackets, heavy parkas, gloves, and hats), though our feet and hands tended to get cold anyhow. At the first of the war, most people did not realize how cold Korea was, and many GIs suffered varying degrees of frostbite before sufficiently warm clothes were provided to all the soldiers stationed there.

Approximately thirty minutes after guard duty began, about twenty-five Korean peasants, wearing traditional white cotton clothes, were spotted walking on the highway with two cattle. Some Koreans had picks and shovels. I wanted to stop them to interrogate them as to who they were and why they were there, but I was prevented by a GI, who told me to let them pass. The peasants approached a destroyed farmhouse, then suddenly disappeared from sight. A few minutes later we heard a series of explosions. We saw several trucks (at least four) from the South Korean Army in flames. The trucks had been carrying ROK soldiers, some of whom were killed with ordnance that the "farmers" had brought down. The explosions not only caused the trucks to explode but propelled about sixty ROK soldiers in the trucks up toward the sky, their bodies burning. The interception of the South Korean soldiers occurred about two hundred yards from the 1st FOB. Needless to say, the explosions woke up most of the soldiers in the 1st FOB. Many ROK soldiers on the ground did not move and appeared to be dead. Many flares emanated from the truck that exploded, revealing that the 1st FOB was surrounded.

By then the GIs were all up and reaching for their rifles in a state of panic. None of the soldiers had any real combat experience and started shooting wildly at anything that moved. Due to their inability to see at night, they were at a real disadvantage. The loud voice that cried, "Don't shoot, we are the ROK Army," was disregarded, and the GIs began to shoot wildly into the darkness. Regardless, the ROK Army started shooting back. After about forty minutes of battle between the ROK Army and the Americans, things settled down, though the Chinese were still shooting flares. The other guard-post soldiers and I retreated to the center of the encampment. The battalion commander requested air support to bomb the enemy position, but support did not materialize until about 7:30 A.M. Air support was very helpful; it largely consisted of fighter planes with small bombs attached to their wings diving into pockets of the enemy position till those pockets of resistance stopped shooting. Everyone was ordered to evacuate except the medics. Under the cover of the air support and the U. N. troops, the 1st FOB evacuated. It took some hours to evacuate, as there were at least sixty ROK troops and twenty GIs dead from the friendly fire. Although I looked frantically for Youngchan, I could not find him. In the meantime, I had to help the medics load the wounded onto the three-quarter-ton truck. I helped load eight wounded soldiers onto the truck and eight soldiers into the ambulance, along with medical equipment. Although the ambulance was designed to carry eight wounded, the medics and I had to stand in the aisle, making it very crowded. It was difficult for the ambulance to move in the uneven field due to snow, ice, and muddy terrain. The other medics and I had to begin pushing the ambulance through the field under fire. Some of the dead soldiers in the ambulance were replaced with soldiers who had been wounded trying to push the ambulance out of the field or who had been discovered as the ambulance was being pushed out.

Finally the medics in their ambulance and their three-quarter-ton truck made it to the main highway. Prior to getting to the main highway, I heard screaming from a minefield. A lone GI had gotten out the night before (presumably to go to the bathroom) and had gotten trapped in the minefield, not realizing at first that it was there. He seemed to be very badly wounded and unable to walk or crawl out of the minefield. Despite the GI's screaming, no one wanted to go into the minefield to rescue him. I volunteered to go into the minefield, although Dr. Tetreaut tried to stop me. I braided a rope from the standing wheat stalks by separating the grass into two separate strands and rubbing the strands together between my hands. Combining the two strands for the length of the grass, the rope was made longer by incorporating additional grass into the two individual strands. I then proceeded toward the minefield.

I did not care if I was killed, figuring that my life span was predetermined and believing that I had lost my family in North Korea. I felt as if I had nothing to lose. I merely prayed to have the strength to pull the man out. I walked into the mine field about seventy feet from the posted sign. I saw the wounded soldier and discovered his field jacket was soaked with blood; blood was running down his face. He was not injured by a mine but had been hit by flying bullets from the friendly fire between the American soldiers and the South Korean Army. I told the man to sit still and started binding the man's feet with rope.

The soldier objected, saying, "What are you doing? I don't want to be pulled out; it's too dangerous."

I replied, "You are too heavy to carry, and you will be killed anyway if you stay here. We must take a chance."

Over the soldier's protests, I dragged him though the minefield and brought him safely to the waiting ambulance despite the bullets that were flying past the both of us. The soldier was loaded into the ambulance without mishap, and the other medics and I were able to continue pushing the ambulance from the field toward the main road. When the enemy bullets died down, the emergency vehicles were pushed out to the main highway. On the highway, the 3rd Army tanks and British tanks evacuated south at about thirty-five miles per hour. There were soldiers on either side of the highway that were pleading for help, but the evacuation line had to keep moving.

Getting back onto the highway, I prepared to shoot toward the enemy fire. An American soldier stopped me, fortunately, as that would have probably drawn more enemy fire. I thought about the "farmers" that I had seen the night before and recognized them as enemy soldiers. I also recognized that the flares used were part of a psychological trick to make the Americans believe they were surrounded by massive numbers of troops.

After 1½ hours of driving, we reached the new encampment of the 1ˢᵗ FOB, having seen my familiar painted sign. During the unloading of the casualties, I worried about Youngchan. I ran to the mess hall and found that Youngchan was serving the GIs food. Unfortunately the corned beef had turned, sickening the soldiers, including the MDs.

Despite the bad food, I could not believe how lucky it was that both of us were alive. Seeing Youngchan at the mess tent moved me to thank my mother's soul for deliverance of both our lives.

A South Korean soldier asked if I could take him to the doctor. I could see his right foot was heavily damaged, shot from toe to heel. Another South Korean soldier with a bloody face appeared with fragments of an exploded mine in his face. (His friend had stepped on a mine while they were retreating.) Although the medics washed the blood from his face and discovered many shrapnel particles, which looked like flies, Dr. Tetreault told him that he could not get at all the fragments, as some were embedded above his eyes. He wrote a ticket to get him transferred to a nearby army hospital.

Despite the hardships, life with the 1ˢᵗ FOB was easier than life in North Korea had been for a long time. Even though Youngchan and I saw each other every day, there was not a lot of time for conversation. I spent most of my free time studying English (ten to fifteen words per day) by the light of a flashlight, time permitting. When Koreans were brought to the hospital, I had to translate. I was encouraged by the GIs to learn English and come to the U.S. To earn extra money toward coming to the U.S., I also washed the doctor's clothes by hand in a creek. This was not too bad a chore in summer, but it was terrible in winter. The nearby creek was nearly frozen, and I had to break the ice to get to the water in the creek. In a typical week, I washed 100-150 pieces of clothing, both for the doctors as well as for other GIs. Clothes dried in freezing weather become very soft after about two to three days. Any extra money I earned (red GI currency, not greenbacks) was transferred into gold rings to prevent currency inflation issues. I carried the gold rings in a pouch around my neck. Much of the money I obtained was given by Youngchan, who played poker at night and won lots of money from GIs.

There were approximately thirty-five people who worked for 1st FOB HQ battery. Of the ones whom I knew personally, five were North Korean civilians: two were college graduates in South Korea; two were college seniors who could not continue their education due to the war; and one worked as a dental assistant. The rest were from South Korea and from many different backgrounds. Aside from the dental assistant and myself, most of the rest of the Koreans were involved with manual labor and were assigned to work for the battery commanding officer. I experienced some jealousy from the other Koreans, as well as the battery commanding officer (captain), because I was not required to do much manual labor. The medical doctors did not permit me to do manual work under the battery CO. The MDs reporting to the battalion CO did not have to accede to the battery CO's request. At one point, the battery CO tried to get me discharged from the outfit because I was not directly reportable to him.

Throughout the three years of service with the Americans, one hazard was the ROK Army, which was very jealous of the Koreans working for the Americans. They knew that the Koreans working for the Americans got regular pay, free meals, free clothing, and free medical care, and that they did not have to participate in combat. The ROK Army was experienced in combat and tried to get bribes from all the Koreans working for the Americans. The ROK Army was constantly on the lookout for young men of draft age whom they could send to the frontlines. Setting foot outside the confines of the 1st FOB meant placing oneself in danger of being drafted into the ROK army on the spot. While I was attempting to obtain an American passport from Pusan or Seoul, I would have a friend do errands relating to this effort, as the friend could travel freely (being forty-five years of age and past draft age). The friend's name was Sok (last name), which means rock in Chinese characters). He was a barber and was a good friend of the father of the girl who I interviewed for marriage in Pyongyang. I didn't want to lead her on, so I told Sok that I was going to the U.S. and didn't know if I would ever come back.

The army doctors whom I worked for included those listed below. Most had attained the rank of captain and had been to medical or dental schools.

Surgeons stayed ten months to a year and then transferred to Japan or the U.S. Other doctors typically stayed a year to a year and a half. Surgeons and dentists typically roomed together in the same tent.

The first doctor was Dr. Theodore Tetreaut from North Carolina. He was about forty years old, very knowledgeable and intelligent, and had been married, divorced, and remarried to a younger woman. He spelled my name as Rhee to correspond to Syngman Rhee instead of Lee or Yi. He often talked to me about French history and other areas, and these conversations helped me improve my English. Friendship with Dr. Tetreaut grew as we retreated back and forth near the Demilitarized Zone, both of us almost getting killed on several occasions. Another employer was the dentist, Dr. Marvin Bonenkamp from southern Missouri. He was in his mid-thirties and very religious. His wife's name was Devli. He was a fast driver, even in a Jeep. He eventually died in a car accident in the U.S., plunging into a ditch. He tried to get me to go to the U.S. and enroll in George Washington University to go to architecture school. However, I couldn't get a scholarship, so I couldn't go to school there.

Dr. Van B. Philpott from Memphis, Tennessee, was another surgeon whom I worked for. He was very tall. His father was also an MD, practicing in Memphis, Tennessee. Dr. Philpott was a graduate of Tulane Medical School in Louisiana. He told me tales about the South, including the specifics of segregation in the South, but assured me that he thought very highly of Asiatic culture.

When he first came to Korea and was assigned to the 1st FOB, Dr. Philpott was introduced to me by Dr. Mossburgh, a dentist who was currently in residence. Dr. Philpott greeted me rather suspiciously at first, perhaps because he had not had many dealings with Korean civilians working for him. I felt as if Dr. Philpott viewed me not as an employee but as a lowly houseboy. Considering the good relations I had managed to maintain with the other doctors on a relatively friendly basis, Dr. Philpott's apparent concerns with rank and class status were worrisome. The first night I spent working for Dr. Philpott was disturbing. At about 2 A.M., he shone a light in my face and asked me where his medical dictionary was. He then asked me to help him find it in his tent. When neither of us could find the dictionary, Dr. Philpott approached Dr. Mossburgh, the dentist from New York, and asked him if he had it. Dr. Mossburgh responded, "Why do you ask me that question? What would I do with it? " Dr. Philpott eventually discharged me to go back to my own tent and went to sleep himself. The next day as I was cleaning up his tent, I found the dictionary in the bottom of Dr. Philpott's sleeping bag. When I presented the dictionary to Dr. Philpott, Dr. Mossburgh thought it was very funny, though I failed to see the humor in it.

Dr. Philpott had a number of requests and ideas that seemed to make life more difficult than it needed to be. One example of Dr. Philpott's fancies included his insistence in taking up the wooden floors inside of all the tents because of his fear of rats that might be hiding under the floor and would spread germs. This did not sit well with the GIs, who had to not only take up the wooden floors, but also had to deal with dirt floors at all times. He also insisted that clothes be washed in the drinking water brought from Seoul instead of creek water. These ideas earned him the name of "Crackpot Philpott." He tended to be very demanding of his Korean houseboys as well until Dr. Mossburgh took him aside and pointed out to him that I, at least, had had a good education under the Japanese and had been a schoolteacher. From that point on, Dr. Philpott took pains to be friendly with me, often taking me on explorations of the battlefield. He was naturally an adventurous sort. However, as a medical officer of a noncombat unit, Dr. Philpott was forbidden from entering a combat zone without permission. Nevertheless, one morning as I was preparing his shaving kit at about 5:30, I saw Dr. Philpott walking toward me with bloody clothes. He told me that he had been in the combat zone and that he had been helping the wounded. He had wanted to see what was happening in the combat zone and was barely able to escape with his life, owing to a fresh infusion of British troops who saved the unit from totally being wiped out by the encroaching Chinese.

One Sunday afternoon he invited me to go by way of a sightseeing expedition on a drive up a hillside on a narrow, dirt road full of potholes with a ditch on either side. In addition to allowing Dr. Philpott to take in some of the local scenery, it also allowed him some practice in driving a Jeep. As the climb got steeper, the Jeep suddenly tipped over. Fortunately both Dr. Philpott and I fell inside the ditch, although we were soaked in oil by the time we got out from underneath the Jeep. After we reached the camp, the Jeep was extracted from the road with some difficulty, and it was heavily damaged.

When Dr. Philpott and I finally reached the camp and word of the damaged Jeep spread, proceedings were instituted to court-martial Dr. Philpott, both for being in a war zone without the permission of his commanding officer and for damaging the new Jeep.

After the court-martial, Dr. Philpott got a Bronze Star for risking his life by trying to help the wounded in the war zone. I never heard whether he was punished for taking the Jeep without permission.

Dr. Guillermo Gonzales was from NYC and was also about forty years old. He spoke with a slight speech impediment and was not fluent in English. He was from Cuba originally and had finished medical school just after WWII in the Bronx section of New York. He was drafted and sent as a surgeon to Korea. The white GIs did not like him, finding both his language and his mannerisms peculiar. However, he recognized a kindred spirit in me and often shared his food parcels (sardines and the like) with me. He also did not know how to drive a Jeep but soon learned with the help of his regular Jeep driver. Once when Dr. Gonzales had to travel to "A" battery, he took me along with him. We were fired upon by snipers, and bullets traveled past our heads as we traveled up the mountain road. Suddenly we heard a loud, growling noise from behind. There was a British tank on our tail, and Dr. Gonzales, in his nervousness, ran the Jeep into a ditch. I managed to avoid injury by jumping from the moving Jeep just prior to the crash. Apart from the Jeep incident, however, I got along very well with Dr. Gonzales, who really was concerned for my welfare.

Dr. Vernon Page, about thirty-five years old, was married to a German immigrant who was about five years older than he was. Dr. Page was an easy-going Texan but was highly sexual and often paid clandestine visits to the nurses' tents that were plying the sex trade. He privately bragged that he had begun having sex at about age nine, though the circumstances were not elaborated upon. Dr. Page always treated me as an equal and did not lie about himself, his background, or the less desirable aspects of life in the U.S. He was not a demanding person, but he also did not do a great deal to help me out in my quest to come to the U.S., although after I finally made it to the U.S., he often invited me to spend the holidays with him.

One cold, snowy night I was asked to go to "B" battery with Dr. Page. I packed both of our gear bags and went with him. Dr. Page went into a tent near "B" battery, and after having been gone about forty minutes, he came out and told me that I should go into the tent and obtain the sexual favors from the nurse that he had already paid for. I declined with thanks, earning me Dr. Page's temporary wrath but possibly saving myself serious health problems.

One night a few months before I tried to come to the U.S., the battery commander tried to fire me. At that point, I was sharing my cot with twenty other Koreans in the same tent. The battery commander sent a notice to me that I was fired due to noncooperation. I believe he did this because I was not really in his direct chain of command and was unavailable for hard-labor efforts. Fortunately my good friend, who was the head of the Korean labor force (and who was also a college graduate from South Korea and w trying to come to the U.S.), was able to talk to Dr. Tom Fleming. Fleming, who was from South Carolina and about thirty-six years old, went to speak to Col. Kinney in the middle of the night. Col. Kinney was upset over this and told the battery commander to stop trying to fire me. Looking back on the affair, I think that my deceased mother must have helped me.

The medical detachment's enlisted men included Frank Welty. He was a very intelligent man — a college graduate who had a journalism degree. When I first met him, he was a corporal and later was promoted to sergeant. Although he was eager to have me tell him about Korean customs and history, he refused to eat Korean or Japanese food. He hated the army and thought that the Korean War was nonsense. When he received a package from his wife, he would usually share it and would share his books with me also. (I especially remember reading a book entitled *Santa Fe*.) However, Frank could be stubborn and challenge authority over trifles. For example, when the GIs went to mess hall, they were required to wear a helmet and carry their rifles. After his promotion, Frank refused to wear his sergeant's stripes. One day he came to the mess hall without his rifle, helmet, or sergeant's stripes. This did not go unnoticed, and he was put on report and forbidden access to the mess hall until such time as he was prepared to conform to the regulations. Youngchan took him food at night till his stubbornness broke and he agreed to wear his sergeant's stripes and helmet and carry his rifle.

Frank Welty undoubtedly saved my life on one occasion. On Christmas Eve, the GIs were allowed to drink some wine and whiskey. I won fifteen dollars for winning the push-ups contest. That night I was approached by an American Indian sergeant who told me to get up so he could shoot me. I was paralyzed with fear. Not wanting to cry out, I resisted the Indian soldier pulling on my arm. Fortunately Frank was able to snatch his gun away and grab the Indian sergeant by the collar and throw him out of the tent.

Elet Wagner was another good friend. One night an American Navy fighter plane dropped friendly fire on the latrine while Elet was teaching me how to drive a Jeep. Elet drove the chaplains between batteries and also helped out with driving the medics around. Elet even introduced a female high school friend as a pen pal for me. Unfortunately I do not remember her name.

Russell Barrett, whose father was the police chief in Washington, D.C., also tried to help me come to the U.S. He wrote to his father, the American embassy, and Catholic University in Washington, D.C., pleading my cause. Although Russell's father invited me to visit Washington, D.C., I discovered that Catholic University was far too expensive for me to even think of attending.

There were twenty-five to thirty-five Koreans working for HQ battery. One reason that the Koreans working for the Americans were so hated by the ROK Army and the South Korean police and would encounter problems when they ventured into the areas outside the American encampments was that the Korean helpers within the military camps were viewed as being lazy predators on the rest of Korean society. Some Koreans behaved badly, taking advantage of Korean widows or those whose husbands were in the army. Many of these women's homes had been damaged or destroyed during the war, and they had one or more children to support. Koreans would take red GI dollars in payment to have clothes washed by the Korean widows but would steal food to pay the Korean women for washing the clothes. The Korean intermediaries would then keep the red GI dollars for themselves.

Sometimes the Korean intermediaries would pretend they were stranded at the Korean women's houses after delivering or picking up the wash on the excuse that there was a curfew that made it impossible for them to return to the Army base. They would then take advantage of the Korean women sexually. They would return to the base bragging of their wonderful sex lives. My brother and I remained apart from this type of conduct, viewing it as both hazardous and unethical, although both of us were viewed as eccentric for not participating in these activities. We were respected by Myong-dong Yi and Kim Yong-Bin for not exploiting the Korean women. Both of these men contracted venereal diseases during their tenure with the 1st FOB.

The six North Koreans who worked for the outfit were all concerned about their families but could not leave the base for fear of the ROK Army. One of my friends who was a houseboy for another captain shot himself in the throat as he was cleaning the gun of the officer whom he was serving, despondent over the loss of his family. It clearly was suicide, as a note was left detailing the reasons for his suicide. The dental assistant tried to save him by providing a transfusion but did not bother to verify his blood type and made a mistake as to the correct vein into which to transfuse the blood. Despite his efforts, the houseboy died, which would probably have been the case in any event.

One day I painted the back of a Jeep over the spare wheel cover using available paint. I painted 1st FOB, Medical Detachment, with the symbol of the 1st FOB, which was Nathan Hale. Many GIs admired my ability at painting, not realizing that I was an experienced artist who had painted many signs, especially when I was teaching school, and had to paint propaganda bulletin boards. The captain who was jealous of me wanted me to paint signs, especially roadside signs, sometimes three-feet by four-feet or two-feet by three-feet. One sign was a three-foot by four-foot sign for 1st FOB depicting a Korean woman nursing a baby and carrying household items on her head, with the GIs looking at the woman's breast with binoculars. It became a very popular sign and was posted at the 38th parallel line. (Although a picture of the sign was rumored to have been published in *National Geographic*, I have been unable to find a copy of it.)

There was a Bob Hope show for the troops at the 1st FOB, as well as other troops, such as the 3rd infantry division and some of the other artillery divisions. This was the first time that I had seen American women apart from missionaries. I thought they were very beautiful, as well as very nice and helpful. The battery commander who disliked me was very vain and took a sponge bath in a dishwashing container in the mess hall in order to make himself more attractive to the women in Bob Hope's cast.

I thought this was very unsanitary but said nothing about it to anyone else. The Bob Hope show was given about twenty miles away from the compound. Dr. Bonenkamp took me there in his Jeep, but we were separated, and I lost track of him prior to the return journey. Luckily I caught a ride back with other troops to a different camp. Leaving that camp, however, I got lost and walked about seven miles before I finally found the 1st FOB.

The R & R taken by the American troops in Korea was helpful to Japan. Each American GI spent about three-hundred to four-hundred dollars in Japan, which the Japanese used to rebuild their country. Troops engaged in active combat were allowed to go to R & R once every six months while those who were not directly involved in combat, such as 1st FOB, were allowed to take R & R once every ten months or a year. There were at least 500,000 GIs in Korea in those days, and the amount of money spent in Japan was considerable. GIs appreciated the friendliness of the Japanese and enjoyed the ability to take baths with the local girls, as well as the massage parlors. (Much money was spent in geisha houses.) The GIs were very fond of Japan, which led to strengthened ties between the U.S. and Japan.

However, GIs who were in Japan often had experiences with prostitutes and came back with gonorrhea or syphilis. The soldiers were supposed to report themselves to the doctors, but many were unwilling to do so. I therefore found myself in the position of having to give antibiotic shots for the VD.

The GIs were helpful in bringing me back items from Japan, mostly gabardine for suits. Also GIs brought me back records from Japan, including a collection of WWII songs, mostly anti-American. At first the store owners were unwilling to sell the records, afraid that the American authorities would cause them to lose their store license. I finally wrote a letter in Japanese explaining the situation, so they finally sold the records to the visiting U.S. soldier.

Another item I wanted was Noritake dishes. Elet Wagner bought the dishes on his R & R visit and had them shipped to his parents' home in Nebraska. (Most of the medics did not visit prostitutes but did visit Japanese restaurants and other points of historical interest.) I retrieved the dishes when I came to the U.S. and have been using them ever since.

Dr. Tetreault was asked a few days later to visit C battery for medical inspection. While at C battery, I was sleeping in his sleeping bag and heard the 3rd artillery battalion shooting at the enemy lines. I was not able to sleep, except for resting my head on the pillow with my left ear exposed. My left ear rang for several days thereafter. I was told that the 3rd artillery group had just received a new batch of guns, and they were doing experimental shooting. (Unfortunately the "experimental shooting" left me with nearly total deafness in my left ear.) The following evening I went into the doctor's tent and tried to light the GI stove. Immediately thereafter Sgt. Russell followed me into the tent and told me to stop firing the stove. He explained that Dr. Tetreault was playing baseball with the other GIs and was hit severely with a bat, which caused internal bleeding. He was then transported to an army hospital in Japan. Sgt. Russell indicated that Dr. Tetreault would not return but that Dr. Gonzales would take his place. I was very sad at this but hoped Dr. Tetreault would be okay. Dr. Tetreault had been very kind to me. The man who had helped everyone out of the combat zone was now ending his career due to a sports accident. A few months later Dr. Tetreault wrote a letter from a hospital in the U.S. He had been promoted to major. Dr. Tetreault said he missed me, but I never received a reply to a letter written in response.

Addendum

It was a rather chilly morning in late November 1952 when the North and South Korean delegates began talking about a cease-fire at Panmunjong. My barber friend (Sok) brought me a copy of a Korean newspaper that he bought from a newspaper stand in Seoul while he was on a three-day leave to visit his family.

The very first thing I noticed on the front page of the paper was that the entire article about the truce talks was written in Hangul (the Korean characters of the phonetic alphabet). Although I had taught school in Pyongyang three years through September 1950 using Korean texts, I was disappointed in my ability to read the paper written with Hangul script only instead of the then-more-conventional script that used a combination of symbolic Chinese characters (called Hanja in Korean, comparable to the Japanese Kanji) mixed with Hangul and had been used during my upbringing in North Korea. The Chinese characters had been used in most Korean writing and literature for centuries, as many Korean words have Chinese character roots. Likewise my early school textbooks were written in a combination of both Chinese and Korean characters. My later school textbooks through the end of WWII were generally Japanese texts written in Hiragana or Katakana, also a form of writing consisting of a combination of Chinese characters and the Japanese phonetic alphabet. Sok explained to me that he could not find any major newspaper printed with Hanja printing. Since the era of King Sejong in the mid-fifteenth century, the use of Hangul was prevalent mostly among women and farmers who found the task of mastering the Chinese characters to be too time-consuming, especially with the native Korean version of pronunciation. King Sejong had sympathy with the commoners, those who had something to say but no means of expressing it, and those who couldn't read charges against them in lawsuits. So King Sejong commissioned scholars to travel throughout Korea, China and Manchuria to gather and organize the sounds they heard. They took several years to do it, and when they finished, King Sejong proclaimed a new alphabet. King Sejong was satisfied with the new alphabet, saying: "Talented persons will learn Hangul in a single morning, and even foolish ones will understand it in ten days. There are practically no sounds that cannot be expressed by Hangul — even the sound of wind and the barking of dogs can be exactly transcribed with it."[1] That's the alphabet that Koreans still use today. As far as the capability of translating most every sound in our living environment, there is one exception to it: There are no Hangul characters that can duplicate the pronunciations for "v" and "th" in the English alphabet.

Despite King Sejong's masterful creation of the Hangul alphabet, the influence of the Yangban (the ruling elite of Korea) and government officials maintained the preference for the Hanmun script in official circles. The Hanmun script allowed the ruling classes to maintain the artistic, literary, and legal traditions created largely by Korean scholars who had received their education in China without reference to the Korean peasants. Although Hangul had been slowly introduced into the official Korean documents since the late 1800s, various influences, including the Japanese occupation, had combined to retain the use of Chinese characters within the Korean writing system, relegating the Hangul system for use with alliterative constructs, including foreign words. Sok indicated that the South Korean educational system had gradually abolished teaching students Chinese characters ever since Korea was liberated from Japan (1945). The South Korean government had wanted to speed up the learning process from elementary school through secondary school by not using such a difficult and time consuming stage as that involving learning Chinese characters for our daily communication.

Just as most European languages have Latin roots for many of their words, many of the Korean and Japanese literary languages are based on Chinese characters (Hanja). Korea and Japan each used their own native, non-Hanja driven words (nouns, verbs, adjectives, adverbs, etc.), which existed in a much earlier era, and integrated them to the Chinese characters for their daily communication.

In contrast to the Chinese characters in which each character represents symbolic expression and meaning, the Korean alphabet is made of twenty-four characters representing sounds and pronunciations. The twenty-four phonetic characters consist of ten vowels and fourteen consonants. By placing the position of each appropriate consonant(s) with respect to the main body of the vowel (either to the left, right, or below), the entire combination then becomes a syllable sound devoid of any symbolic meaning. Including the main vowel, a maximum of four characters can be placed in each syllable. Likewise the vowels themselves can be grouped together to produce different sounds, such as ahya, yo, yu, ae, eh, ye, etc. If any identical consonants are lined up side by side, the sound of the consonants become much stronger or high-pitched. For example, when the two consonants of "z" (ㅈ) are lined up side by side, they will be pronounced as the "zz" (ㅈㅈ) of pizza in English. Likewise two s's placed together (ㅅㅅ) will sound like the "s" of sun in English. In my opinion, there is no other country on the continent that uses strong/high-pitched sounds in its daily language as much as is true of Korean. A Wall Street Journal article from September 11, 2009 ("To Save its Dying Tongue, Indonesian Isle Orders Out for Korean"), a discussion is provided about a school teacher in the Indonesian island of Buton (named Abidin) who is attempting to render the Cia-Cia language into Hangul in order to preserve it. Other languages where this has been attempted have been for languages spoken in Nepal, as well as Lahu, a language spoken in China and Southeast Asia.

Except for the Hangul characters of hissing or tooth sounds, such as "s," "z," or "ch," the scripts of consonants and vowels contain mostly images of square or rectangular patterns (either whole or partial), similar to those used in the paper-backed, decorative ribs of old Korean sliding doors, as illustrated in the following characters:

ㄱ, ㄴ, ㄷ, ㄹ, ㅁ, ㅂ, ㅏ, ㅑ, ㅓ, ㅕ, ㅗ, ㅛ, ㅜ, ㅠ, ㅡ, ㅣ
(k) (n) (d) (r) (m) (b) (ah) (ya) (eo) (yeo) (o) (yo) (u or oo) (yu) (uh) (i)

In spite of the splendid creation of the phonetic alphabet (Hangul), the use of Chinese scripts in Korean literature did not phase out until after WWII. The following paragraphs explain the reasons for the continued existence and use of the Hanja-driven words in Korean-written script and language.

Although the process of learning Chinese characters is lengthy and difficult, it has many advantages of use in both verbal and written communications once learned. I myself learned to read and write — through my grandfather — one thousand Chinese characters with Korean pronunciation at age six. I also learned the same one thousand characters with Japanese pronunciations in the Japanese elementary school system. After the third grade, the Japanese board of education in Korea did not allow students to read or possess any Korean newspapers or textbooks in school, as we were expected to converse in Japanese and write in Japanese Kanji. By the time I reached fourth grade, I was able to read nearly 70 percent of Kanji scripts in Japanese newspapers. It should be noted that the Japanese Kanji differs from Korean Hanja in that the former has two different ways of pronouncing a Kanji character: the "On" mode of pronunciation and the "Kung" mode of pronunciation. The "On" mode represents the sound of a single syllable, which is usually quite similar to the Chinese and the Korean pronunciations. The "On" mode is used mostly in the literary language of poets and writers, whereas the "Kung" represents one or more syllables per character using the pronunciation(s) of colloquial Japanese words that are mostly used for ordinary communications or as the name of a person. Under the Kung mode, there are many different ways of pronouncing a single Kanji character. Nonetheless, both the "On" and "Kung" modes can be used simultaneously in any written script or in conversations. For an example:

朝日 (Kanji): あさひ (asa hi, read in "Kung"mode); ちょうにち (chonichi, read in "On"mode). Both translations mean "morning sun."

As mentioned previously, the symbolic character of the Hanja script has its unique and intrinsic meaning. A reader could quickly grasp the entire meaning or content of script written in an ordinary page of 150 to 200 words in less than a minute; in Hangul a reader is required to read word by word (or line by line for an inexperienced reader) to understand the entire script. The advantage of using Hanja is that more meaning is conveyed in fewer words. However, there is a certain disadvantage in using Chinese characters without mixed use of the native words in Korean or Japanese literature. It does not have as much flexibility in using prefixes, suffixes, prepositional phrases, conjunctions, and sentence endings (such as the "is" in English), which is described as "nita" in Korean or "desu" in Japanese. For this reason, even for twentieth-century literature most Korean or Japanese writings used a combination of both Hanja for nouns, verbs, adjectives, adverbs, and Hangul (Korean alphabet) or Hiragana/Katakana (Japanese alphabet) for the phrases mentioned above. Fortunately the grammar structures of both Korean and Japanese languages were nearly the same at the time when I was in school. My fifth grade Japanese teacher once told us in class that since the grammar structures between Chinese and English were so similar, it was easier for a Chinese person to learn English than it was for a Korean or Japanese person to learn English.

In comparing the use of Hanja-driven spoken words, which are usually closely related to a similar Chinese word, versus pure Korean native words, the former conveys a level of meaning, whereas the latter does not give any such atmosphere or appreciation during ordinary conversation. Here are some examples:

The name of the North Korean capital (Pyongyang) in Chinese characters is written as 平壤, meaning "flat land region." However, the Korean alphabet denotes nothing except for the phonetic pronunciation of the name. Particularly for the younger generation of Koreans, it's difficult to understand how and what the name of Pyongyang actually represents. The truth is that about 85 percent of Korea is mountainous or hilly. Fortunately Pyongyang was one of a few flat places in Korea that the ruling class of centuries ago thought could be suitable to establish a capital in the Northern region or a commercial trading center. In modern usage, although the name Pyongyang is derived from a Hanja word, its transliteration into Hangul divests it of its inherent, symbolic meaning.

Similarly I was once introduced to a coworker at the American medical detachment in South Korea who was from Chung Chon Do province. I immediately expressed my respectfulness toward him and acknowledged that he was from an area where many people of either literary or military fame had been born and served ancient Korea for many centuries. In Hanja, "Chung" means loyalty, dedication, or faithfulness. However, the meaning of the name loses its character when transliterated into the phonetic Hangul. For a younger generation who does not have any training in Hanja, it can only think of the province as "just another name," not recognizing its intrinsic meaning, which remains hidden from them.

During the Japanese occupation in Korea (1910-1945) and dating back to the beginning of the Yi era (1392), the name of my native country was called Choson (in Korean) or Choseng (in Japanese). If this word is written in Chinese characters, it means "the land of morning calm." At the time of the creation of this name, our ancestors believed that Korea was located in the eastern region of the earth, and they would get the benefit of living in a peaceful, morning atmosphere.

The name of the United States in Hanja is written as 米 國 and pronounced as "Mikuk"in Korean and "Beikoku" in Japanese. These characters are simply translated as "rice country." Immediately after WWII, the South Korean government decided to change the Hanja script by keeping the same pronunciation of "Mikuk" to 美國, meaning "beautiful country." The government completely abolished the written name of "rice country," 米 國. Because there is some conflict in the two different ways of writing and pronouncing the name of the U.S. in Japanese, my guess is that they are still using the name "Beikoku" — or simply call it "America."

Like many other Korean girls who were born during or after the Japanese occupation, a famous Korean singer has the name Mija. The direct translation of the Hanja for her name is "beautiful child." Again, this does not carry intrinsic meaning in Hangul or as a pure Korean word, except that the name identifies a person whose name is known as a famous singer.

Finally the name of the Pacific island Iwo Jima is rendered in Chinese characters as "sulfuric island" or "volcanic island." Without knowledge of the Chinese script, a majority of young Koreans think of the name only as the island in the Pacific that went through the most intensive battle between the American Marines and the Japanese soldiers."

Nowadays most South Koreans use native Korean words and phrases in conversation, as well as in written script, in preference to Hanja-driven words. If there is no other choice but to use the Hanja-driven words, these words would also be incorporated in conversation or in written scripts with the Korean alphabet, but the majority of the older folks still prefer to use the Hanja characters when writing.

Let us bring out few examples of the above two kinds of words:

English	Hanja-driven word (partial or whole)	Traditional Korean word
Twenty years old	I (pronounced as ee) ship sae	Sumusal
City park	Shi naekongwon	None
Beautiful girl	Minyo	Arumdaunyoza, "yoza" is also a Hanja-driven word
Country (nation)	Kuk	Nara
Parents	Bumo	Abojiwa Omoni
East	Dong	None

Here are some translations of the names of automobiles or electronic products produced in Korea or in Japan that are mostly driven from Hanja or Kanji.

Name of product	Meaning
Hyundai	Modern era
Samsung	Three stars
Mazda	Poor farm (or rice paddy)
Isuzu	Rock lake
Toyota	Rich farm (or one's last name in Japan)
Nissan	Japanese product (or Made in Japan)

In conclusion, South Koreans have been using Hangul (Korean alphabet) exclusively in their publications regardless of whether the words are native Korean words or Hanja-driven words. Many native Korean words do not have Hanja equivalents and vice versa. On the other hand, North Koreans had been using a mixture of both Hanja and Hangul in their publications for a number of years even after WWII, but recent indications are that they also use Hangul extensively in their current publications. Perhaps because the educational system in North Korea wants to promote more scientific learning and other important fields of study rather than to put so much effort into learning Hanja, a greater emphasis on Hangul has been implemented. Furthermore, perhaps the North Korean government wanted to promote consistency in the pattern of communication between North and South Korea. Although King Sejong the Great created one of the most accurate, phonetic alphabets in the world nearly 550 years ago, use of the Hanja in written scripts did not cease in Korea until recent decades. I believe it is due to the fact that many famous Korean scholars (entirely men in those days) were educated in China. The Yi-Choson's dynasty (1392-1910) greatly rewarded the scholars who were educated and received degrees from China, perhaps because such education was costly and viewed as the benchmark of society. Such education was rigorously tested both before the students were allowed to leave China, as well as prior to receiving an appointment at the Korean court. As a result, the highly educated scholars continued to use Hanja in keeping with their efforts to maintain an unbroken line of continuity of the Chinese-derived literary and cultural traditions, as well as their own government documents.

There was a famous song composed for a woman whose husband was on his way to China to be a "great scholar." The name of the song is "Arirang." Even after many centuries have passed, this song is not only sung individually but also at the opening or closing of most musical festivals in Korea. In recent years, it has been sung at the Pyongyang auditorium by the musical performers of both North and South Korea with a hopeful gesture toward the impulse for Korean reunification. Typically the song is written all in Hangul with traditional Korean words. The first part of the song can be read and translated as follows:

아리랑아리랑아라리요아리랑고게로넘어간다.

(Arirang, Arirang, arariyo. Arirangkogeroneommoganda).

나를벌이고가시는님은, 십리도못가서발병난다
(Narulbeorigokashinunnimmn, shimridomotkaseobalbyongnanda!)

Translation:

Oh, Arirang (the name of the hillside where the couple lived), Oh Arirang, please listen, Arirang. My husband is crossing over the hills of Arirang.

He who abandoned me and is leaving me, will be suffering from feet wounds before he reaches twenty-four miles.

The following list is a translation or meaning of words used in this chapter:

Word	Translation	Country used in
Hangul	Korean phonetic alphabet	Korea
Hanja	Chinese symbolic character or letter	Korea
Kanji	Chinese symbolic character or letter	Japan and U.S.
Hanmun	Script written in Chinese characters using hanja	Korea
Katakana	Japanese alphabet, mostly used in adapted Japan foreign words or names and some scientific names	Japan
Hiragana	Japanese alphabet, commonly used in parts of a script, except where katakana and/or Kanji apples	Japan

Chapter IX
Leaving Korea and Going to the U.S.

When the top U.S. military brass visited the 1st FOB and other detachments, all the Koreans were asked to make the area more presentable. They worked to make roads more passable by filling in potholes and more attractive by outlining roads with rocks that were painted white. The appearance of high-ranking military officers seemed to augur the end of the war sooner rather than later.

Processing Application to the U.S. while with the 1st FOB

I very much wanted to come to the U.S. to study. This desire had long predated my association with the 1st FOB, and I had been encouraged in this ambition by my father despite all the obstacles, especially after the mess that the Communists had made of North Korea. The political situation in North Korea would have placed travel to the U. S. or any other Western nation completely beyond the realm of possibility had it not been for my travels south during the Korean War. North Koreans were required to get permission to travel between towns; traveling to other countries was completely out of the question for the average person. No citizen of North Korea was allowed past the 38th parallel for any reason.

I started making serious plans to come to the U.S. in July 1952, which was when I began processing my application in earnest. Although I had spent most of my off-hours studying English in preparation ever since I began working for the 1st FOB, my actual paperwork processing did not begin till July 1952.

Although our contact with Americans in North Korea had been limited to our occasional interactions with the missionaries there, we saw that the immense hatred borne by the Communists for the U.S. probably had its roots in envy, as the U.S. had been able to produce a standard of living that the Communist governments could not begin to achieve. Although the Communist propaganda had railed against the dog-eat-dog aspects of capitalism, GIs within the compound spoke as if the U.S. was a utopia and did not allude to its less desirable aspects, though many GIs questioned the purpose of the war and their roles in it. Mainly they were homesick and adrift in an alien culture.

Coming to the U.S. required both a visa as well as a passport, both of which required numerous approvals from various governmental agencies. I was fortunate in my employment in that my employers, i.e., the various doctors for whom I worked, including Col. Kinney, permitted me considerable latitude in taking time off to try to obtain the necessary governmental approvals for my paperwork.

In July 1952, I was strongly encouraged to come to the U.S. by Elet Wagner, Dr. Bonenkamp, Frank Welty, Dr. Philpott, Dr. Gonzales, and Russell Barrett, each of whom provided me with a large measure of support, both personal and sometimes financial. Russell Barrett mostly took care of paperwork sent to the American embassy at Seoul or Pusan (the southern tip of Korea), where the American embassy was located at one point. In order to come to the U.S. to study, I required a sponsor to ensure the U.S. government that I would not become a welfare case. Elet Wagner got his father to find a sponsor who owned the Goodyear Tire store in Hastings, Nebraska. Elet also got me a one-year scholarship to Hastings, Nebraska.

Besides getting the visa and passport, however, there were other obstacles. Only 5 percent of the total authorized immigrants to the U.S. at that time were from Asia. Competition for slots in the quota was very severe and usually was extended to the sons and daughters of the South Korean elite, who were able to come to the U.S. six months or so after the passport application. In contrast it took me more than two years to obtain all the required signatures. Seeing the amount of time required away from base and the difficulties associated in obtaining the needed signatures, Youngchan did not feel as if it were worthwhile for him to also obtain a visa and passport, as he probably would have lost his job with the 1ˢᵗ FOB. He chose to wait to try to come to the U.S. some years later when I was well-established in my chosen career in the U.S.

One of the major barriers to entry into the U.S. was my prior background as a teacher in North Korea, as the South Koreans, and possibly the Americans, initially suspected me of being a North Korean agent. Under the ordinary course of things, had I not been able to join up with the 1ˢᵗ FOB, I would have been drafted by the ROK into the army and sent to the frontlines to fight against the North Koreans.

I had managed to save up my wages from the 1ˢᵗ FOB, from washing clothes, and from Youngchan's gambling earnings, which totaled four thousand dollars in red GI money. The money saved up went into my duffel bag, which Russell Barrett watched while I went to Seoul and Pusan to try to arrange for my paperwork to the U.S. There was no freedom of travel between 1ˢᵗ FOB and Seoul and Pusan due to patrols by ROK Army and the police. The Koreans who were in the refugee camp in Pusan worked hard to survive. They flattened beer cans and created metal sheets to augment the ability of the canvas to keep out the rain, sun, and wind. The GIs — trying to be helpful — donated provisions of powdered eggs and powdered milk. Unfortunately the eggs and milk made the Koreans sick, so they wound up throwing the entire lot into the ocean.

I was picked up by the ROK Army and/or police more than a dozen times. (Police in the cities (Seoul and Pusan) and the ROK Army between the 1ˢᵗ FOB and the cities were constantly on the lookout for young men of draft age to send to the front. I had several near misses at being forced to serve in the ROK Army.) For the first part of the paperwork, Sok was able to deliver the paperwork to the Korean government or the U.S. embassy. Col. Kinney was able to write a letter that would provide a letter of introduction, which sometimes served to stave off the ROK Army and the police, sometimes not.

Another obstacle in obtaining a visa from the Korean government was a lack of knowledge in Korean history, for which I was required to pass a test. The test at the U.S. embassy was mostly in English. Each time I was captured and put in jail led to a diminution of speech, which was another concern.

The Korean government did not want to send students to the U.S. unless it was for engineering and if it was assured that the student would return to Korea. Passports lasted for four years, and visas were for two years only. The ability to study nontechnical subjects overseas was nearly nil.

In order to get a passport approved, at least thirty signatures were needed from various South Korean government agencies. Signatures from the ministry of defense, ministry of the interior, as well as police chiefs, were required. Each signature required at least two to three weeks to obtain, and each signature required a separate trip from the relative safety of the 1st FOB to the government agency.

The reason for the Korean history test was that the Korean government was concerned that each student represent Korean history proudly. Another requirement was to prove that the student had graduated from middle school or college. A visa application required that the applicant pass a physical, as well as an English test, most of which were conducted using *Reader's Digest* as a reference. I also had to pass a background check; I was investigated thoroughly by the Central Intelligence Committee, which was located in Korea and questioned all soldiers and other Koreans with whom I had been in contact since coming to South Korea.

Thankfully Col. Kinney and others were patient with the amount of time required for me to complete the processing of my paperwork. Other GIs, even those not associated with the 1st FOB, helped in providing rides throughout South Korea. Travel between Seoul and Pusan was largely via train.

My teacher's college certificate was required to demonstrate that I had fulfilled the visa requirement to have attended middle school. I managed to obtain a duplicate certificate by going to a reunion in Seoul of the teacher's college alumni. I saw many of my former classmates, as well as the former dean of the school. I mentioned the need of a teacher's college certificate to my former dean, who assured me it would not be a problem. Somehow he managed to obtain a duplicate certificate of my graduation certificate. The dean also mentioned the fact that he had met with Choi Ingun from North Korea, my previous friend from the teacher's college.

After about a year, I had obtained about two-thirds of the signatures required. A friend from the 1st FOB volunteered to take me to meet his uncle, who was a member of the Korean Parliament. His uncle provided a fancy dinner, and his aunt provided a bed for the night. The uncle owned the Hotel Bando, which served mostly Americans.

On one of my trips to Pusan while I was attempting to get a visa signature from the ministry of defense, I happened to meet an engineer in the hotel where I had been staying. The ministry of defense had previously been unwilling to provide a signature for my passport application due to my age and susceptibility to the draft. However, my acquaintance had studied in the U.S. and was able to provide me a letter of introduction, in which he requested that the ministry of defense sign my application. A half hour later I had the required signature and was on my way back to the 1st FOB.

Riding the train between Seoul and Pusan left me open to questioning and search by the ROK Army and the police. The MPs would check each car, requesting to see identity cards from each passenger. On my last trip to Pusan to take the English test at the American embassy, I had to pretend I was going to the men's room and had to hang on the outside of the train, traveling between cars while it was in motion. I made it to the men's room without problem, which fortunately was not checked by the MPs.

After taking the English test, the return from Pusan occurred at night in the dark. I did not want to hang on the outside of the train as I had done previously and decided that if I were caught, that that would be the end of it and that my dreams would have to go by the board at last. Fortunately a kindly farm woman spotted my worried face, guessed I was attempting to evade the MPs, and suggested that I lie on the floor next to her. She covered me with quilts and laid her baby on top of the quilts, effectively shielding me from the MPs.

After the harrowing ride from Pusan, I needed to get back to the 1st FOB. Fortunately I was able to get a ride in a truck from the 3rd Infantry Division going halfway to the 1st FOB. Unfortunately, however, the truck driver let me off right in front of a ROK Army post. Right away the South Koreans caught me and forced me to stay overnight. I was put in a small pup tent (four foot by six foot) with a straw floor and no mattress. It was terribly cold in the tent, and there were ticks in the straw. The next day I was presented to the lieutenant in charge. The lieutenant was sympathetic to my plight but decided to leave my disposition up to the guard who had captured me. I was able to bribe the guard with all the money I had in my pocket (about fifteen dollars), as well as a bottle of sake that I had been bringing back as a present for a member of the 1st FOB. Fortunately I was able to hitch another ride with a military supply truck, which took me within two miles of the 1st FOB.

When I returned to the 1st FOB, there was great consternation on the part of the battery commander, who was most displeased about the fact that I had been away from the post, as well as the fact that he had lost a good deal of money to my employer, Dr. Vernon Page, in a poker game.

Having gotten nearly all the signatures required for my visa, I felt somewhat more secure. The Americans were mass bombing Pyongyang, and Syngman Rhee was asked to step down due to the corruption of his regime. Youngchan saw him walking toward the airport in order to leave the country despite the offers of the police to drive him there.

Overnight the Korean government suddenly changed currency. My Korean friend offered to change the red GI currency through the offices of his Uncle Oh, who was still in Parliament. However, when my friend did not return, I knew I had been swindled.

I was left with little money for a number of days. I mentioned the story of my loss of red dollars to my friends in the medical detachment. However, I still had the gold rings that I previously had accumulated. Elet Wagner managed to collect money from the GIs to help me go to the U.S., using his helmet as a collection plate. Elet managed to collect one thousand dollars for my transportation to the U.S.

After the money donation, all the medics were rotated back to the U.S. New medics were also helpful in raising cash, and my efforts to travel were made considerably easier by the gradual diminishment of hostilities on the Korean peninsula. I was able to visit my uncle in Seoul also. My visa was finally granted by the U.S. embassy in 1954.

I had to get a complete physical and receive many different immunization shots. Since I had had my visa granted, I felt more secure, though I still had my speech impediment, which was undoubtedly of psychological origin and due to the many hardships I had experienced over the past few years. Nevertheless, I left the 1st FOB at the end of February 1954 amidst a great farewell party.

I had a choice of buying a plane ticket or a ship ticket and chose the latter since it was $300 versus $750 for a plane ticket. It took approximately one week to travel between Pusan and Seattle, Washington. I brought two suitcases to Seoul. Sok was there and wanted to take me to a prostitute. I chose to lay down on top of her with a quilt between us. I managed to obtain a climax, but I did not want to have actual intercourse with her for fear of contracting some disease. I gave her two gold rings by way of recompense.

I went for a last visit to my uncle; he gave me supper and cautioned me to be nice to all the Americans I met. I also had dinner with my friend Choi and caught up on the news about Miss Rhee and the lady teacher with whom I had guarded the school. Although I had the opportunity to renew acquaintance with Miss Rhee, and possibly Sok's daughter, I chose to make it to the ship before the U.S. government changed its mind. Just prior to leaving Pusan, I sold the gold rings I had accumulated and refreshed my supply of cash. This time there was no currency conversion, and I managed to keep my hands on enough cash to get started in the U.S.

I took a cargo ship between Pusan and Seattle. A porter helped me onto the ship with my luggage, and to the dismay of my new cabin roommate, I did not tip the porter, being unaware of the tipping custom that was expected of me. The new cabin roommate wasted no time in telling me about the tipping that would be expected of me as I traveled —and when I was located in the U.S. Sok saw me off at the pier and wished me well. Traveling between Pusan and Seattle, Washington, took approximately one week. Although I was invited to dine every evening at the captain's table, I seldom was able to eat more than a few mouthfuls before having to excuse myself to heave the contents of my stomach over the side of the ship. I experienced several bouts of seasickness, especially when traveling past the Aleutian Islands, where the waves were high and choppy. The ship undertook an evacuation exercise to ensure passenger safety in the event of a mishap. I happened to catch sight of Adzu Island, where two thousand Japanese died due to American artillery bombing (called "Fall of Jewel" or "Kyoksai"), as we went past.

After a rather rough sea journey, I arrived at Seattle on March 14, 1954, at about 9 P.M. The skipper asked me to join him on a walk down the pier. The skipper was dressed up, and the skyline was imposing. We went to a restaurant and rode in an elevator, which contributed to my queasiness. I had not yet gotten my "land legs" and still felt prone to seasickness, even on land.

After dinner the skipper and I headed back to the ship at about 11 P.M. The skipper offered to take me to San Francisco at no additional charge, but I wanted no part of more time on the ship. I wanted to travel for awhile on the train and visit Dr. Marshall Atkinson, who was then practicing in San Francisco.

I tried to unload my gear the next day from my hotel room but found myself very weak. This time I remembered to leave money for the room service and took the train through Oregon to San Francisco. I was duly impressed by the scenery of the Northwest, finding it much more impressive than Korean scenery. Dr. Atkinson's wife picked me up at the San Francisco train station and took me to Dr. Atkinson's home.

Dr. Atkinson had two children: a boy (five years old) and a girl. When Dr. Atkinson arrived home that evening, he and I discussed my recent sea voyage and what had happened since I had last seen him 3½ years earlier. I had been writing letters to Dr. Atkinson in the interim so that he knew that I was coming to the U.S.

I was given a spare bedroom upstairs for a few days amidst close scrutiny by the children, one of whom wanted me to stay permanently. Dr. Atkinson gave me some suits for retailoring although the doctor was much taller than I.

During the next four days, I visited San Francisco as a tourist. I learned to ride the streetcar and visit the zoo, which was located in a park-like atmosphere with large, healthy spruce trees and an animal-confinement area that seemed to provide the animals a great deal of free space, comparable to their natural habitat.

Dr. Atkinson also took me to his office where he practiced ophthalmology. His office on the top floor of his office building allowed a view of the entire city of San Francisco, including the bay and the Golden Gate Bridge, as well as the Berkley campus of the University of California. Dr. Atkinson took me down to the bay, where I was able to view the fishermen getting ready to take their boats out into the harbor and watch the seagulls ply the shore. The breakers pounded the beach heavily, and the air was cold, as it was the end of March.

After touring San Francisco, I took the Burlington Zephyr to Lincoln, Nebraska, which was ninety miles from Roseland, Nebraska, a town of about 150 people. Elet's father, Fred Wagner, ran the gas station in Roseland, in combination with an auto repair shop, and was well-known and liked by everyone in Roseland.

After arriving at the train station in Lincoln, I had to wait for the bus to Hastings, Nebraska. A beautiful young woman of about eighteen years of age asked me where I was going. She was curious about me since I was one of the few Orientals she had seen. She had just graduated from high school and was looking for a job. She lived with relatives, her parents having died years earlier. Her name was Martha Long. She was very friendly and was quite different from Korean girls in that she spoke freely and frankly and did not avert her head when talking to me.

Harold Wagner came to pick me up at the Hastings bus station. He was a man of about 350 pounds and was probably about 33 years of age. Prior to leaving Hastings, Harold drove me through the Hastings College campus so that I could see where I would be going to school the following year. It was a small, Presbyterian school with about five buildings and one church; it very well kept with large elm trees. There were three dormitories for men and one for women.

Harold drove to Roseland in what seemed to me to be an excessive rate of speed, about sixty miles per hour. (In all my years of riding in Jeeps, I had seldom traveled more than thirty-five miles per hour!) Additionally it seemed likely that with all the cornstalks on either side of the road, we might very well get hit by a vehicle pulling out from a side road.

The first stop in Roseland was Elet's father's house. Elet was very pleased to see me and introduced me to his fiancé, Beverly. Later I would meet my sponsor, Mr. Baldwin, who owned the Goodyear Tire store in Roseland. Although Mr. Baldwin signed the paper as my sponsor, he was never required to support me financially.

Elet's mother was in her mid-fifties. She was a very gracious lady who demonstrated her concern for my welfare by ensuring I had sufficient blankets and quilts for my bed in the attic, where I shared a room with Elet's brother Paul (who had just graduated from high school), and by making sure I got to eat things that I enjoyed.

Harold lived in a different house since he was married. But he took me to many different friend's houses in the nearby towns in the evening when time allowed. When I was not visiting Harold's friends, I watched TV in my attic bedroom, my favorite programs being wrestling shows.

Elet's family played a major role in the United Methodist Church in Roseland and took care of the church building. In gratitude I painted a picture of Christ in the Garden of Gethsemane (eight feet by six feet). I painted the picture in the auto repair garage, and Harold took it a few months later to have it framed. To the best of my knowledge, the picture still hangs in the church.

Fred Wagner helped me out by finding me various odd jobs, such as painting windows with lettering for commercial purposes and truck painting. The odd jobs helped out for paying for expenses at Hastings College, as well as for living expenses with Mr. and Mrs. Wagner.

With all the excitement and new environment, my speech ability improved, and my voice returned to normal. In the fall of 1954, I moved into Broncs Hall at Hastings College and painted a sign to put at the front of my dormitory. The sign was featured in a local newspaper.

All the Wagner children had attended Hastings College. Because the college was small, it did not offer engineering degrees. It was largely a liberal arts college that also featured theatrical, journalism, and theology degrees. Although it offered calculus, differential equations, and physics, it did not offer a full suite of technical classes. I knew I would have to transfer elsewhere sooner or later. Most of the classes in math and science were ones I had already had in the teacher's college in Pyongyang. Fortunately the professors worked to help me overcome my English deficiency.

There were approximately twenty foreign students on the campus: Six were from Korea and the rest from Taiwan, central Europe, and Africa. Most of the students were liberal arts majors except for two girls who were studying science (pre-engineering).

The business organizations and CEOs of nearby businesses (building and manufacturing companies, mostly) invited the students to dinner about once a month. They asked the students to speak about their home countries and cultures and published the results of the meetings and photographs in the local papers. In those days, the Nebraska farm communities had a lively interest in the exotic Far Eastern cultures, deeming them very different from their own. The Nebraska folks were surprised at how similar the Korean culture was to the U.S. culture in many respects.

In February, Elet's mother prepared a special birthday dinner for me. She even prepared rice, but the rice was cooked with milk, which made it hard to swallow and produced indigestion the next day due to my lactose intolerance.

There was one incident during the summer that involved the lone Korean girl who was studying pre-engineering at Hastings. She came from a well-to-do family and had been involved with a U.S. lieutenant who had promised to marry her when she came to the U.S. Although he had arranged for her to attend Hastings College, when she finally came to the U.S., she discovered that he had already married a local girl. She was understandably bitter at this, but she was an excellent student in math — at the top of her class. She accepted my offer of a date, but as I didn't have a car and didn't know the Western conventions of dating (opening car doors, pulling out chairs at the dining table), she was not interested in me — besides the fact that I had very little money. Also the other Korean men were interested in her as well, so she decided not to continue seeing me. Thereafter I decided not to pursue Korean girls and stick to American girls, who were less stuck-up.

Toward the end of the semester, Dr. Philpott called from the University of Wisconsin. He was working as a research pathologist at the University of Wisconsin hospital. He asked whether I would be interested in transferring to the University of Wisconsin campus at Madison. I was concerned about my lack of money, but Dr. Philpott offered me a job as a lab technician working in the laboratory where he worked.

Dr. Philpott told me not to worry about money, as he was sure that the lab technician's job would pay for my expenses. I would be working on a special program under Dr. Philpott and Dr. Strowitz that was well-funded. Dr. Strowitz was the head of the research lab. The lab was doing research on irreversible hemorrhagic shock, which would often occur when wounded soldiers experienced excessive bleeding during the first thirty minutes of transportation from the battlefield. Both Dr. Philpott and Dr. Strowitz were also involved in biochemical research work that involved pathogens that would cause diarrhea in North Korean troops, making them too weak to fight.

Dr. Strowitz wanted to find a cure for the irreversible hemorrhagic shock. Dr. Strowitz agreed to hire me as an assistant to Dr. Philpott in the research program. I would be working as a half-time assistant at the rate of $150 per month. That was not enough to take care of the tuition; however, I was able to get a half-time scholarship through a program that had been set up through U.S. Representative Carl Thompson. I accepted the offer and transferred from Hastings College to the University of Wisconsin.

Concern over the competition in the engineering school was foremost in my mind. The first-two-year dropout rate was 50 percent of initial enrollment. Only 25 percent graduated from initial enrollment.

After undergoing some interim tests, I received a letter of acceptance from the University of Wisconsin. It took over two years to get a passport from the Korean government while the University of Wisconsin required only two months to process an application. I was delighted to be in the U.S., where there seemed to be far less corruption than in Korea. My ambitions seemed to be in a place that would allow them to be harnessed. Also I was given free speech therapy for a year and a half.

Thereafter while I attended the University of Wisconsin engineering school, my former friends and associates invited me for holidays and vacations. They sent me money as gifts at Christmas and, in the case of Dr. Gonzales, enabled me to find a temporary summer job in NYC. The most memorable visit that I made was to Frank Welty's summer home in Estes Park, Colorado. The Rocky Mountains remind me of home in Pyongyang and seem to be the place where I feel most comfortable. Within a three-day period of time during the early 1950s, Frank and I hiked all over the Mummy Range — me in tennis shoes carrying a seventy-five-pound army duffel bag. We hiked twenty miles per day for three days.

Looking back over the past years, I feel as if my dreams came true. Feelings of loss for my family still remain, however. For all the painful moments of loss, things have come out better than expected — with my deceased mother's help.

Endnotes
1. Elizabeth Pond, "The Korean Alphabet — It's Easy," *The Christian Science Monitor*, October 16, 1974.

Bibliography

"Amaterasu," https://en.wikipedia.org/wiki/Amaterasu.

Aoki, Hiroshi. *Recent History of Japan, China and Korea*. Japan: Gentosha, 2003. (日本、中口、朝鮮；近現代史；青木裕司)

Bull, Andy. "The Sports Blog." *The Guardian.co.uk*. 27 August 2011.

Halberstam, David. *The Coldest Winter: America and the Korean War*. New York: Hyperion, 2007.

Hastings, Max. *The Korean War*. New York: Simon and Schuster, 1987.

"Imperial Regalia of Japan," https://en.wikipedia.org/wiki/Imperial_Regalia_of_Japan.

"Joseon," http://en.wikipedia.org/wiki/Joseon

Kibaek, Yi. The New Theory of Korean History. Seoul: Samshin Munhwa Publication. (韓國史新論, 口基白, 三信文化社)

"Kim Il-Sung," https://en.wikipedia.org/wiki/Kim_Il-Sung.

Knight Ridder News Service-Washington. *Denver Post*. 1983, Section D.

Kuliak, S. and J. Clarke, ed. "Museum Guide." The Art Institute of Chicago: 1992.

Pond, Elizabeth. "The Korean Alphabet — It's Easy." *The Christian Science Monitor*. 16 October 1974, 10.

Stone, I.F. *The Hidden History of the Korean War*. Second Modern Reader Paperback Edition. New York and London: Monthly Review Press, 1971.

"To Save its Dying Tongue, Indonesian Isle Orders Out for Korean." *Wall Street Journal*. 9 September 2009.

Weintraub, Stanley. *MacArthur's War: Korea and the Undoing of an American Hero*. New York: The Free Press, 2000.

"Yamata no Orochi," https://en.wikipedia.org/wiki/Yamata_no_Orochi.

Yi Soon Shin videotapes. Vol. II, Disk 3, Episode 25.

My oil painting of my house and its surroundings, where I took daily morning exercise in my youth age.

Three closest medic friends and I in front of Battalion First Aid Station.

Youngchan and his 4 daughters celebrating Chusok.

My last day of service at Battalion Medics (March 13, 1954) before leaving to come to the U.S.

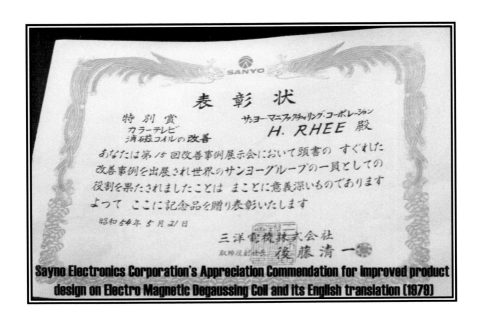

Sanyo Electronics Corporation's Appreciation Commendation for improved product design on Electro Magnetic Degaussing Coil and its English translation (1979)

3855562

THE UNITED STATES OF AMERICA

TO ALL TO WHOM THESE PRESENTS SHALL COME:

Whereas, THERE HAS BEEN PRESENTED TO THE

Commissioner of Patents

A PETITION PRAYING FOR THE GRANT OF LETTERS PATENT FOR AN ALLEGED NEW AND USEFUL INVENTION THE TITLE AND DESCRIPTION OF WHICH ARE CONTAINED IN THE SPECIFICATION OF WHICH A COPY IS HEREUNTO ANNEXED AND MADE A PART HEREOF, AND THE VARIOUS REQUIREMENTS OF LAW IN SUCH CASES MADE AND PROVIDED HAVE BEEN COMPLIED WITH, AND THE TITLE THERETO IS FROM THE RECORDS OF THE PATENT OFFICE IN THE CLAIMANT (S) INDICATED IN THE SAID COPY, AND WHEREAS, UPON DUE EXAMINATION MADE, THE SAID CLAIMANT (S) IS (ARE) ADJUDGED TO BE ENTITLED TO A PATENT UNDER THE LAW.

NOW, THEREFORE, THESE Letters Patent ARE TO GRANT UNTO THE SAID CLAIMANT (S) AND THE SUCCESSORS, HEIRS OR ASSIGNS OF THE SAID CLAIMANT (S) FOR THE TERM OF SEVENTEEN YEARS FROM THE DATE OF THIS GRANT, SUBJECT TO THE PAYMENT OF ISSUE FEES AS PROVIDED BY LAW, THE RIGHT TO EXCLUDE OTHERS FROM MAKING, USING OR SELLING THE SAID INVENTION THROUGHOUT THE UNITED STATES.

In testimony whereof, I have hereunto set my hand and caused the seal of the Patent Office to be affixed at the City of Washington this seventeenth day of December, in the year of our Lord one thousand nine hundred and seventy-four, and of the Independence of the United States of America the one hundred and ninety-ninth.

Attest

Attesting Officer

C. Marshall Dann

Commissioner of Patents

Me in my school uniform of Pyongyang Teachers College.

Uncle Eu, my mother's younger brother, deceased late 1955.

Studying English inside a bunker with a flashlight, preparing for the test at the American Embassy for visa grant, 1954

Park Moranbong, Pyongyang. View from the base of hill, including restaurants and Buddhist temples.

Taedong Gate, Pyongyang, where I and my brother went through the gate December 20, 1950, and started evacuating toward Seoul, South Korea, as refugees.

Panoramic view of Park Moranbong and Nung-nado Isle. The bridge was destroyed during the Korean War.

Structure, Ulmildae at top of Park Moranbong, Pyongyang. In July 1894, this area was under an intensive battle ground for Japan-China War.

Medical Personnel, Capt. Bill G. Choi, Corporal Balboa and I

My best friend, Choi, from Pyongyang. Last dinner gathering before I left Korea for the U.S.

My passport picture, applied through South Korean government to come to the U.S.

My roadside painting for the U.S. Battalion I served

My parallel bar exercise, Korean War front

One of my signs painted on the back of a Jeep for the Army surgeon I worked for

Elet W. and his wife at Roseland, Nebraska. Elet and his father helped me a great deal to come to the U.S.

My senior year at the University of Wisconsin, School of Engineering, 1961

My first day's arrival at Hastings, Nebraska, where I attended my first year of college in the U.S..

Army surgeon Capt. Bill G. (right) and dentist, Capt. Marvin B.

Christmas Party with the medics of Medical Detachment, 1952.

Dr. Bill G. and I in front of an ambulance

The first settlement of our Battalion Headquarters after retreating from the Chinese offence.

Korean civilian employees at the U.S. army camp I served, December 1950-March 1954

Clearing rocks in the cold rapid stream for laundry.

Push up contest with G.I.s at Christmas party, 1952.

Lockheed Martin Astronautic's Appreciation Award for work on Atlas V Launch vehicle program for NASA (2001).

SANYO

Certificate of Commendation
May 21, 1979

Special Award

Sanyo Manufacturing Corporation

Modification and improvement
of Magnetic Degaussing Coil
for color television

To: Mr. H. Rhee

For the 15th Exhibition relating Product Improvement and modification, you have presented/demonstrated outstanding work on the above component used in color television. As an individual of the Global Sanyo Group, you have achieved your duty with a deep significance. Thus, I am presenting you this certification of commendation and sending you a memorial gift.

Vice President
Sanyo Electronics Corporation, Japan

(Singed with seal)

Park Hee Byung's grave marker in Riverside Cemetery, Denver, Colorado

Hackchan prays at the grave of Park Hee Byung

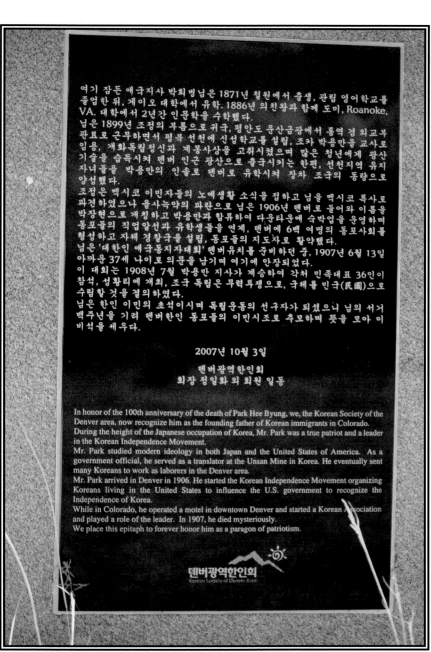

여기 잠든 애국지사 박희병님은 1871년 철원에서 출생, 관립 영어학교를
졸업한 뒤, 게이오 대학에서 유학. 1886년 의친왕과 함께 도미, Roanoke,
VA. 대학에서 2년간 인문학을 수학했다.
님은 1899년 조정의 부름으로 귀국, 평안도 운산금광에서 통역 겸 외교부
관료로 근무하면서 평북 선천에 신성학교를 설립, 조카 박용만을 교사로
임용, 개화독립정신과 계몽사상을 고취시켰으며 많은 청년에게 광산
기술을 습득시켜 덴버 인근 광산으로 출국시키는 한편, 선천지역 유지
자녀들을 박용만의 인솔로 덴버로 유학시켜 장차 조국의 동량으로
양성했다.
조정은 멕시코 이민자들의 노예생활 소식을 접하고 님을 멕시코 특사로
파견하였으나 을사늑약의 파란으로 님은 1906년 덴버로 들어와 이름을
박장현으로 개칭하고 박용만과 합류하여 다운타운에 숙박업을 운영하며
동포들의 직업알선과 유학생들을 연계, 덴버에 6백 여명의 동포사회를
형성하고 자체 경찰국을 설립, 동포들의 지도자로 활약했다.
님은 '대한인 애국동지자대회' 덴버유치를 준비하던 중, 1907년 6월 13일
아까운 37세 나이로 의문을 남기며 여기에 안장되었다.
이 대회는 1908년 7월 박용만 지사가 계승하여 각처 민족대표 36인이
참석, 성황리에 개최, 조국 독립은 무력투쟁으로, 국체를 민국(民國)으로
수립할 것을 결의하였다.
님은 한인 이민의 초석이시며 독립운동의 선구자가 되셨으니 님의 서거
백주년을 기려 덴버한인 동포들의 이민시조로 추모하며 뜻을 모아 이
비석을 세우다.

2007년 10월 3일

덴버광역한인회
회장 정일화 외 회원 일동

In honor of the 100th anniversary of the death of Park Hee Byung, we, the Korean Society of the
Denver area, now recognize him as the founding father of Korean immigrants in Colorado.
During the height of the Japanese occupation of Korea, Mr. Park was a true patriot and a leader
in the Korean Independence Movement.
Mr. Park studied modern ideology in both Japan and the United States of America. As a
government official, he served as a translator at the Unsan Mine in Korea. He eventually sent
many Koreans to work as laborers in the Denver area.
Mr. Park arrived in Denver in 1906. He started the Korean Independence Movement organizing
Koreans living in the United States to influence the U.S. government to recognize the
Independence of Korea.
While in Colorado, he operated a motel in downtown Denver and started a Korean Association
and played a role of the leader. In 1907, he died mysteriously.
We place this epitaph to forever honor him as a paragon of patriotism.

덴버광역한인회
Korean Society of Denver Area

Close-up of the Park Hee Byung grave marker.